U.S. Constitution
RHYMES
Volume 2

*Side-by-Side
Constitution in Rhymes
For All Ages*

Debbi S. Rollo

First Edition

U.S. Constitution Rhymes
Volume 2
Side-by-Side
Constitution in Rhymes
For All Ages

by Debbi S. Rollo

Published by Debbi S. Rollo Orem, UT 84057

ISBN: 979-8-9852508-2-4

www.readconstitution.com
Email Debbi at drollo1787@gmail.com

Contents

ARTICLE 1

ARTICLE 1 continued

ARTICLE 1 continued

ARTICLE 2

ARTICLE 3

ARTICLE 7

CHAPTER FOUR – *Amendments to the Constitution (1-27)*

CHAPTER FIVE – *Resources*

CHAPTER SIX – *Workbook Section*

From the Author

The Constitution of the United States of America is one of the greatest and most important documents ever written. The first three words, "We the People", affirm that the government of the United States exists to serve its citizens.

The Constitution spells out the laws, limits, rights, and resolutions that outline how our government works. It is vital to know and understand how it was set-up, how it is supposed to run, and know our rights so that we can defend them.

It is also imperative that we know what is and what is *not* constitutional so we, as citizens, can hold government officials accountable and vote for those who will keep their oath to support and uphold the U.S. Constitution.

Living in a free society without being restricted by an oppressive government is vital to exercising our unalienable rights of LIFE, LIBERTY, and THE PURSUIT OF HAPPINESS. It is the life blood of each person born on earth and what we are endowed to be – free!

The Constitution of the United States can be hard to understand. I believe that in order to truly learn and love something, we need to understand it. The U.S. Constitution is worth learning and loving. That is why I wrote this book, a simple translation of every single Article, Section and Clause, through rhymes, of all seven Articles and the twenty-seven Amendments.

It is the duty and privilege of each American citizen, especially the rising generation, to know what it means to be free and how to defend and maintain our liberty.

Thomas Jefferson said, "Educate and inform the whole mass of the people…They are the only sure reliance for the preservation of our liberty." It is my hope and deep desire that we will wake up to the importance of preserving our liberty before it is too late. It begins with studying the U.S. Constitution!

CHAPTER ONE

About the Constitution

THE CONSTITUTION

The Constitution gives us laws,
Meant to keep us free,
Filled with rules and regulations,
For our liberty.

SUPREME LAW

The Constitution is,
The Supreme Law of the land,
Yet it must have limits,
Which is why it's grand!

LAWS
The U.S. Congress makes laws,
For the United States,
Made of the House and Senate,
Of elected delegates.

THE STATES
Rights are reserved to the States,
And "We the People" too,
Have both checks and balances,
To keep things just and true.

THREE BRANCHES
Executive, Judicial,
The Legislative too,
Three branches of government,
Will guide our country through.

SEPARATE POWERS
Three separate branches,
In this great land of the free,
Have separate powers,
With their own authority.

HANDS OF A FEW
Our founding fathers learned,
That power should not be,
In the hands of a few,
But spread out separately.

A REPUBLIC
People elect those to represent,
The people and their State,
Our government is a Republic,
A system that is great!

CHECKS AND BALANCES

We have checks and balances,
The VOTE we have too,
So power is allotted,
To more than just the few.

SENATOR

A Senator's elected,
So they can represent,
Their State in the Congress,
With the people's consent.

FREEDOM, EQUALITY, JUSTICE

Freedom, equality,
And justice for all,
Was our Founding Fathers'
Vision, creed, and call.

CHURCH AND STATE
The separation between,
Church and State was made,
For freedom of religion,
Which should never fade.

IF YOU CAN KEEP IT
What kind of government,
Ben Franklin once was asked,
Did you give the people,
For which you were tasked?
It is a Republic,
Ben Franklin replied,
If you can keep it,
With hope, he implied.

ORIGINAL CONSTITUTION

Where is the original
U.S. Constitution now?
At the National Archives
In Washington D.C. – Wow!

RESTORE THE CONSTITUTION

Let's restore the Constitution,
To its meaning and rightful place.
Let's stand up for rights and freedom,
With conviction, strength and grace.

CHAPTER TWO

Preamble to the Constitution

"We the People of the United States, in Order to form a more perfect Union, establish Justice, insure domestic Tranquility, provide for the common defense, promote the general Welfare, and secure the Blessings of Liberty to ourselves and our Posterity, do ordain and establish this Constitution for the United States of America."

AN INTRODUCTION

The Preamble is,
An Introduction to,
The U.S. Constitution,
Of rights for me and you!

A FRAMEWORK

The Preamble is a framework,
For a just government,
To establish peace and justice,
Designed with this intent.

WE THE PEOPLE
"We The People" are great words,
With joy shout and sing!
Power comes from the people,
Not Congress or a King!

POWER LIES IN
We the People,
We the People,
Is where the power lies.
In the U.S.,
In the U.S.,
For freedom we must rise.

MORE PERFECT UNION
A more perfect union,
A nation of liberty,
To establish justice,
And insure tranquility.

COMMON DEFENSE

To protect America,
A national defense,
Is provided to secure,
Our Safety; which makes sense!

PROMOTE GENERAL WELFARE

To promote general welfare,
Means those elected should,
Make laws for our well-being,
To keep things running good.

BLESSINGS OF LIBERTY

The Government is to secure,
The Blessings of Liberty.
They must protect my rights and those,
Of my Posterity.

ESTABLISHED AND ORDAINED

Our U.S. Constitution,
Founding fathers have proclaimed,
Is by and for the people,
Established and ordained.

CHAPTER THREE

Articles of the Constitution (1-7)

ARTICLES OF THE CONSTITUTION
The purpose of the Articles,
Is very plain to see,
To establish government,
In order to be free.

Article 1: Legislative Branch
Article 2: Executive Branch
Article 3: Judicial Branch
Article 4: States' Powers
Article 5: Amendments
Article 6: Federal powers
Article 7: Ratification

CAN AND CANNOT DO

How do we know what Government
Can and cannot do?
Article One, with ten sections
Is an overview.

TEN SECTIONS

Article One has ten sections,
Ten sections to explain,
Powers granted to government,
With limits to maintain.

ARTICLE 1

ARTICLE 1, Section 1

All legislative Powers herein granted shall be vested in a Congress of the United States, which shall consist of a Senate and House of Representatives.	<u>A CONGRESS</u> There is a Congress, States Article One, Two separate powers, Now isn't this fun! One is the Senate, Representing their State, The other, the House, With new laws to create.

ARTICLE 1, Section 2, Clause 1

The House of Representatives shall be composed of Members chosen every second Year by the People of the several States, and the Electors in each State shall have the Qualifications requisite for Electors of the most numerous Branch of the State Legislature.	<u>HOUSE OF REPRESENTATIVES</u> The House of Representatives, Are elected, it appears, By the people of their State, Elected every two years.

ARTICLE 1, Section 2, Clause 2

No Person shall be a Representative who shall not have attained to the Age of twenty five Years, and been seven Years a Citizen of the United States, and who shall not, when elected, be an Inhabitant of that State in which he shall be chosen.

ELECTED TO THE HOUSE

You must be at least twenty-five,
Yes, twenty-five years old,
To be elected to the House,
In Section Two we're told.
You must have been a Citizen,
Of the United States,
For at least seven years,
So Section Two dictates.

LIVE IN THE STATE

To be elected to the House,
You must live in the State,
The State in which you're chosen.
Now don't you think that's great?

ARTICLE 1, Section 2, Clause 3

The 14th Amendment, Section 2 changed how people are counted

*Representatives and direct Taxes shall be apportioned among the several States which may be included within this Union, according to their respective Numbers, which shall be determined by adding to the whole Number of **free Persons**, including those bound to Service for a Term of Years, and **excluding Indians** not taxed, **three fifths of all other Persons**.*

*The actual Enumeration shall be made **within three Years** after the first Meeting of the Congress of the United States, and within every subsequent Term of **ten Years**, in such Manner as they shall by Law direct.*

***The Number of Representatives** shall not exceed one for every thirty Thousand, but each State shall have at Least one Representative; and until such enumeration shall be made, the State of New Hampshire shall be entitled to chuse three, Massachusetts eight, Rhode-Island and Providence Plantations one, Connecticut five, New-York six, New Jersey four, Pennsylvania eight, Delaware one, Maryland six, Virginia ten, North Carolina five, South Carolina five, and Georgia three.*

This part was changed by the Fourteenth Amendment

TEN YEARS

Americans are counted
Every ten years or so,
In a census, to keep track
So government will know.
The number represented
By the House, they need to know,
Which helps determine taxes,
While the population grows.

INDIANS AND SLAVES

The Indians were not taxed,
So they were not counted.
And slaves, three-fifths a person,
When this law was founded.

WITHIN THREE YEARS

People in the United States,
Will be counted within three years,
After the first meeting of Congress,
To number Representatives.

ARTICLE 1, Section 2, Clause 4

When vacancies happen in the Representation from any State, the Executive Authority thereof shall issue Writs of Election to fill such Vacancies.	VACANCY If a State Representative, Leaves office or they die, The Governor of that State, Calls an election, why? To elect another one, To take their place, of course, This is the grand procedure, The Founders did endorse.

ARTICLE 1, Section 2, Clause 5

The House of Representatives shall chuse their Speaker and other Officers; and shall have the sole Power of Impeachment.	POWER TO IMPEACH The House of Representatives, Has sole power to impeach. They also elect the Speaker, Who quite often gives a speech.

ARTICLE 1, Section 3, Clause 1

The Senate of the United States shall be composed of two Senators from each State, chosen by the Legislature thereof, for six Years; and each Senator shall have one Vote.

The 17th Amendment changed this rule. Instead of Senators being chosen by the Legislature, the people vote for Senators.

TWO SENATORS
Two Senators are elected,
From each State, it's true.
Two Senators serve for six years,
From each State, yahoo!

SENATORS KNOCKING
Two Senators,
Knocking at the door.
Two Senators,
Standing on the floor.
Two Senators,
Elected by their State.
Two Senators,
Are called to legislate.

ONE VOTE
Oh listen up,
And clear your throat,
The Senators
Each have one vote.

SENATOR AMENDMENT
The 17th Amendment changed
The Senator Election rule.
Instead of State Legislatures,
The *people* vote for them; how cool!

ARTICLE 1, Section 3, Clause 2

Immediately after they shall be assembled in Consequence of the first Election, **they shall be divided as equally as may be into three Classes.** *The Seats of the Senators of the first Class shall be vacated at the Expiration of the second Year, of the second Class at the Expiration of the fourth Year, and of the third Class at the Expiration of the sixth Year, so that one third may be chosen every second Year;* **and if Vacancies happen by Resignation, or otherwise,** *during the Recess of the Legislature of any State, the Executive thereof may make temporary Appointments until the next Meeting of the Legislature, which shall then fill such Vacancies.*

ONE-THIRD OF SENATORS
Each of the Senators,
Can serve a six year term.
One-third are elected,
Every two-years, we learn.

IF A SENATOR RESIGNS
What happens if a Senator,
Resigns or if they die?
The Governor picks someone else,
'Til next election time.

The 17ᵗʰ Amendment
Changed this rule.

ARTICLE 1, Section 3, Clause 3

No Person shall be a Senator who shall not have attained to the Age of thirty Years, and been nine Years a Citizen of the United States, and who shall not, when elected, be an Inhabitant of that State for which he shall be chosen.

TO BE A SENATOR
To be a Senator,
A person must be,
A U.S. Citizen,
And over thirty.
For at least nine years,
That person must have been,
In order to serve,
A U.S. Citizen.

ARTICLE 1, Section 3, Clause 3 (continued)

No Person shall be a Senator who shall not have attained to the Age of thirty Years, and been nine Years a Citizen of the United States, and who shall not, when elected, be an Inhabitant of that State for which he shall be chosen.	<u>LIVE IN THE STATE</u> A Senator must live, They must live in the State, Where they were elected, To serve and legislate.

ARTICLE 1, Section 3, Clause 4 & 5

The Vice President of the United States shall be President of the Senate, but shall have no Vote, unless they be equally divided. *The Senate shall chuse their other Officers, and also a President pro tempore, in the Absence of the Vice President, or when he shall exercise the Office of President of the United States.*	<u>PRESIDENT OF THE SENATE</u> The President of the Senate, Is Vice President indeed, But only votes if there's a tie, A reason to intercede. And if the Vice President, For some reason can't be there, Then the Senate gets to choose, Now doesn't that seem fair?

ARTICLE 1, Section 3, Clause 6

The Senate shall have the sole Power to try all Impeachments. When sitting for that Purpose, they shall be on Oath or Affirmation. When the President of the United States is tried, the Chief Justice shall preside: And no Person shall be convicted without the Concurrence of two thirds of the Members present.	<u>IMPEACHMENT TRIALS</u> The Senate has power over, Impeachment trials, you see. They must all swear to tell the truth, And two-thirds must agree.

ARTICLE 1, Section 3, Clause 7

Judgment in Cases of Impeachment shall not extend further than to removal from Office, and disqualification to hold and enjoy any Office of honor, Trust or Profit under the United States: but the Party convicted shall nevertheless be liable and subject to Indictment, Trial, Judgment and Punishment, according to Law.	**NOT RE-ELECTED** If one's impeached and convicted, Re-elected they can't be, Or cannot be re-appointed, But can be tried by a jury.

ARTICLE 1, Section 4, Clause 1

The Times, Places and Manner of holding Elections for Senators and Representatives, shall be prescribed in each State by the Legislature thereof; but the Congress may at any time by Law make or alter such Regulations, except as to the Places of chusing Senators.	**ELECTION TIMES AND PLACES** The State Legislature gets to pick, Election times and places, But Congress can make changes to, Their plans in certain cases.

ARTICLE 1, Section 4, Clause 2

The Congress shall assemble at least once in every Year, and such Meeting shall be on the first Monday in December, unless they shall by Law appoint a different Day *This was changed by the 20th Amendment. Members of Congress will meet at least once each year on January 3rd.* *Or they can choose a different day.*	**MEET ONCE A YEAR** The Congress will meet, At least once every year, To talk about laws, So there's no need to fear.

ARTICLE 1, Section 5, Clause 1

Each House shall be the Judge of the Elections, Returns and Qualifications of its own Members, and a Majority of each shall constitute a Quorum to do Business; but a smaller Number may adjourn from day to day, and may be authorized to compel the Attendance of absent Members, in such Manner, and under such Penalties as each House may provide.	**MEET REGULARLY** To serve in their elected seat, The House and Senate need to meet, With each other regularly, Or they could face a penalty.

ARTICLE 1, Section 5, Clause 2

Each House may determine the Rules of its Proceedings, punish its Members for disorderly Behaviour, and, with the Concurrence of two thirds, expel a Member.	**KICK MEMBERS OUT** Both the House and the Senate, Each make up their own rules, And they can kick members out, If they behave like fools. If two-thirds of them vote to, Kick them out, they will. So be true, good, and honest On Capitol Hill!

ARTICLE 1, Section 5, Clause 3

Each House shall keep a Journal of its Proceedings, and from time to time publish the same, excepting such Parts as may in their Judgment require Secrecy; and the Yeas and Nays of the Members of either House on any question shall, at the Desire of one fifth of those Present, be entered on the Journal.	**KEEP A JOURNAL** Each House keeps a journal, Of what's done and said, And it can be printed, So it can be read.

ARTICLE 1, Section 5, Clause 4

Neither House, during the Session of Congress, shall, without the Consent of the other, adjourn for more than three days, nor to any other Place than that in which the two Houses shall be sitting.	<u>MORE THAN THREE DAYS</u> While each House is in Session, They are required to stay, And they must get permission, To leave for more than three days.

ARTICLE 1, Section 6, Clause 1

The Senators and Representatives shall receive a Compensation for their Services, to be ascertained by Law, and paid out of the Treasury of the United States. They shall in all Cases, except Treason, Felony and Breach of the Peace, be privileged from Arrest during their Attendance at the Session of their respective Houses, and in going to and returning from the same; and for any Speech or Debate in either House, they shall not be questioned in any other Place.	<u>PAID BY THE GOVERNMENT</u> The House of Representatives, And Senators as well, Get paid by the Government. Do you think that's swell? <u>CANNOT GET ARRESTED</u> Except for disturbing the peace, For stealing or treason, The Senate or the House member, No matter the season, Cannot get arrested, While work is being done, So explains Section Six, Of Article One.

ARTICLE 1, Section 6, Clause 2

No Senator or Representative shall, during the Time for which he was elected, be appointed to any civil Office under the Authority of the United States, which shall have been created, or the Emoluments whereof shall have been encreased during such time; and no Person holding any Office under the United States, shall be a Member of either House during his Continuance in Office.	**OTHER GOVERNMENT OFFICE** If you are serving in Congress, You're not allowed to work, Somewhere else in the Government, That would be berserk!

ARTICLE 1, Section 7, Clause 1

All Bills for raising Revenue shall originate in the House of Representatives; but the Senate may propose or concur with Amendments as on other Bills.	**ALL BILLS BEGIN** All Bills begin in the House, To raise taxes (money), But remember, the Senate, Must then also agree.

ARTICLE 1, Section 7, Clause 2

Every Bill which shall have passed the House of Representatives and the Senate, shall, before it become a Law, **be presented to the President of the United States**; *If he approve he shall sign it, but if not he shall return it, with his Objections to that House in which it shall have originated, who shall enter the Objections at large on their Journal, and proceed to reconsider it. If after such Reconsideration two thirds of that House shall agree to pass the Bill, it shall be sent, together with the Objections, to the other House, by which it shall likewise be reconsidered, and if approved* **by two thirds of that House, it shall become a Law.**

But in all such Cases the Votes of both Houses shall be determined by yeas and Nays, and the Names of the Persons voting for and against the Bill shall be entered on the Journal of each House respectively. If any Bill shall not be returned by the President within ten Days (Sundays excepted) after it shall have been presented to him, the Same shall be a Law, in like Manner as if he had signed it, unless the Congress by their Adjournment prevent its Return, in which Case it shall not be a Law.

IF A BILL PASSES

If a Bill passes House and Senate,
Then it goes to the President.
If it is signed, then it becomes law,
With no further argument.
If the President won't sign the Bill,
Then they write down reasons why,
Send it back to the House or Senate,
To give it another try.

THE SAME BILL AGAIN

If two-thirds of House and Senate,
Vote for the same Bill again,
Then the Bill becomes a law,
Which for them is a big win!

ARTICLE 1, Section 7, Clause 3

Every Order, Resolution, or Vote to which the Concurrence of the Senate and House of Representatives may be necessary (except on a question of Adjournment) **shall be presented to the President of the United States**; *and before the Same shall take Effect, shall be approved by him, or being disapproved by him,* **shall be repassed by two thirds** *of the Senate and House of Representatives, according to the Rules and Limitations prescribed in the Case of a Bill.*

PRESIDENT MUST SIGN
The President must sign,
Every law that's passed,
By the House and Senate,
Isn't that a blast!

VETO
If the President won't sign,
A Bill, it's a veto,
Then a two-thirds vote must pass,
To make it law, you know!

ARTICLE 1, Section 8

LEGISLATION

Legislation – making laws,
Only Congress can do,
With limits from Section eight,
Article One, its true!

ARTICLE 1, Section 8, Clause 1, 2 & 3

*The Congress shall have **Power To lay and collect Taxes**, Duties, Imposts and Excises, to pay the Debts and provide for the common Defence and general Welfare of the United States; but all Duties, Imposts and Excises shall be uniform throughout the United States;* *To **borrow Money** on the credit of the United States;* *To **regulate Commerce** with foreign Nations, and among the several States, and with the Indian Tribes;*	<u>POWER TO TAX</u> Congress has power to tax, Spend, borrow, and regulate Commerce with other nations, Indian tribes and States.

ARTICLE 1, Section 8, Clause 4

To establish an uniform Rule of Naturalization, and uniform Laws on the subject of Bankruptcies throughout the United States;	<u>CITIZENSHIP AND BANKRUPTCIES</u> Rules for Citizenship, And Bankruptcies belong, To Congress to make laws, That keep our country strong.

ARTICLE 1, Section 8, Clause 5

To coin Money, regulate the Value thereof, and of foreign Coin, and fix the Standard of Weights and Measures;	<u>MONEY, WEIGHTS, AND MEASURES</u> Congress can coin and regulate, The value of money; sweet! And standardize Weights and measures, Such as pounds, inches, and feet.

ARTICLE 1, Section 8, Clause 6

To provide for the Punishment of counterfeiting the Securities and current Coin of the United States;	COUNTERFEIT Congress has the power to, Punish those who counterfeit. Printing money is a crime, That the law will not permit.

ARTICLE 1, Section 8, Clause 7

To establish Post Offices and post Roads;	POST OFFICES AND ROADS The Congress shall establish, Post offices and roads, To send and receive letters, And drive with heavy loads.

ARTICLE 1, Section 8, Clause 8

To promote the Progress of Science and useful Arts, by securing for limited Times to Authors and Inventors the exclusive Right to their respective Writings and Discoveries;	SCIENCE AND THE ARTS Your invention, the book you write, Or picture that you draw, Is your legal right to own, Protected by the law. To promote the progress, Of Science and the Arts, Congress gives protections, For freedom to impart.

ARTICLE 1, Section 8, Clause 9

To constitute Tribunals inferior to the supreme Court;	**COURTS** Courts are set up by Congress, Throughout the whole country, Lower than the Supreme Court, For truth and liberty.

ARTICLE 1, Section 8, Clause 10

To define and punish Piracies and Felonies committed on the high Seas, and Offences against the Law of Nations;	**ON THE SEAS** What happens on the high seas? Are there laws out there? Yes, and Congress makes them, So pirates should beware!

ARTICLE 1, Section 8, Clause 11

To declare War, grant Letters of Marque and Reprisal, and make Rules concerning Captures on Land and Water;	**DECLARE WAR** Congress has power to declare war, And make rules on land or sea, About the capture of people, Or capture of property.

ARTICLE 1, Section 8, Clause 12

To raise and support Armies, but no Appropriation of Money to that Use shall be for a longer Term than two Years;	**RAISE AND SUPPORT ARMIES** Congress has power to raise armies, Power to pay for them too. But no longer than two years, That's what this law says to do.

ARTICLE 1, Section 8, Clause 13

To provide and maintain a Navy;	**A NAVY** Congress has the power, To create a Navy, And also pay for it, In our military.

ARTICLE 1, Section 8, Clause 14

To make Rules for the Government and Regulation of the land and naval Forces;	**RULES FOR GOVERNMENT** The Congress makes rules, For the Army, For the Government, And the Navy.

ARTICLE 1, Section 8, Clause 15

To provide for calling forth the Militia to execute the Laws of the Union, suppress Insurrections and repel Invasions;	**STATES' NATIONAL GUARD** Congress has power, To act in this regard: To call upon the States' National Guard. They can stop riots, Enforce National laws, And fight invaders, According to this Clause.

ARTICLE 1, Section 8, Clause 16

To provide for organizing, arming, and disciplining, the Militia, and for governing such Part of them as may be employed in the Service of the United States, reserving to the States respectively, the Appointment of the Officers, and the Authority of training the Militia according to the discipline prescribed by Congress;	**APPOINT AND TRAIN** Congress has power to organize, The National Guard (state army). States appoint and train their officers, With the proper authority. Congress has power to organize, The militia (state army), And supply weapons that they need, With the States' authority.

ARTICLE 1, Section 8, Clause 17

To exercise exclusive Legislation in all Cases whatsoever, over such District (not exceeding ten Miles square) as may, by Cession of particular States, and the Acceptance of Congress, become the Seat of the Government of the United States, and to exercise like Authority over all Places purchased by the Consent of the Legislature of the State in which the Same shall be, for the Erection of Forts, Magazines, Arsenals, dock-Yards, and other needful Buildings;—And	**THE U.S. CAPITOL** Congress will be in charge of, A place, no more than ten miles square, For the Government to work, A place of freedom in the air. Congress will be in charge of, This great place of liberty, It's the U.S. Capitol, Now in Washington, D.C.!

ARTICLE 1, Section 8, Clause 18

To make all Laws which shall be necessary and proper for carrying into Execution the foregoing Powers, and all other Powers vested by this Constitution in the Government of the United States, or in any Department or Officer thereof.	**ALL LAWS** Congress shall have the power, To make all the laws it needs, Under the Constitution, For our Nation to succeed.

ARTICLE 1, Section 9, Clause 1

The Migration or Importation of such Persons as any of the States now existing shall think proper to admit, shall not be prohibited by the Congress prior to the Year one thousand eight hundred and eight, but a Tax or duty may be imposed on such Importation, not exceeding ten dollars for each Person. *The Thirteenth Amendment Banned Slavery*	### SLAVE TRADE Congress can't stop the slave trade, 'Til at least eighteen-o-eight. A tax of up to ten dollars, Can be charged; that is the rate. ### SLAVERY BANNED The Thirteenth Amendment Banned slavery, my friend. It took a while, but finally Slavery was condemned.

ARTICLE 1, Section 9, Clause 2

The Privilege of the Writ of Habeas Corpus shall not be suspended, unless when in Cases of Rebellion or Invasion the public Safety may require it.	### WRIT OF HABEAS CORPUS The Writ of Habeas Corpus, A fundamental right, is thus: Protection from permanent, Unlawful imprisonment. ### PUT IN JAIL People who are put in jail, Must be told why they are there, Unless it's from rebellion, To be just and to be fair.

ARTICLE 1, Section 9, Clause 3

No Bill of Attainder or ex post facto Law shall be passed.	**BILL OF ATTAINDER** "No Bill of Attainder shall be passed." What is this law about? You can't be guilty of a crime, Without a trial, no doubt. **GUILTY OF A CRIME** A person can't be guilty, And punished for a crime, Without having a trial, Because of Section Nine! **EX POST FACTO** "No ex post facto Law shall be passed," Is a strange sentence indeed. Article One, Section Nine states, It's a right that's guaranteed. If you did something legal, That was legal at the time, But later that same law changed, You're not guilty of that crime.

ARTICLE 1, Section 9, Clause 4

No Capitation, or other direct, Tax shall be laid, unless in Proportion to the Census or Enumeration herein before directed to be taken. *Changed by the 16th Amendment*	**TAXES BASED ON CENSUS** Congress must tax, based on Number of citizens, Counted on the census, Says this law herein. **COULD TAX** The Sixteenth Amendment, Changed this law to say, Congress could tax people, In whatever way.

ARTICLE 1, Section 9, Clause 5

No Tax or Duty shall be laid on articles exported from any State.	**TAX FROM ONE STATE TO ANOTHER** Congress can't tax things, Sold from one state to another, Even if you buy Them from your Aunt or Brother.

ARTICLE 1, Section 9, Clause 6

No Preference shall be given by any Regulation of Commerce or Revenue to the Ports of one State over those of another: nor shall Vessels bound to, or from, one State, be obliged to enter, clear, or pay Duties in another.	**PORTS AND SHIPS** Congress can't treat one port, Better than the rest, That is favoritism, If you haven't guessed. And no ship from one state, Can get taxed, you know, For using another, State's port if they go.

ARTICLE 1, Section 9, Clause 7

No Money shall be drawn from the Treasury, but in Consequence of Appropriations made by Law; and a regular Statement and Account of the Receipts and Expenditures of all public Money shall be published from time to time.	**MONEY TO BE SPENT** Congress must pass a law, For money to be spent, And then from time to time, There must be a statement.

ARTICLE 1, Section 9, Clause 8

No Title of Nobility shall be granted by the United States: And no Person holding any Office of Profit or Trust under them, shall, without the Consent of the Congress, accept of any present, Emolument, Office, or Title, of any kind whatever, from any King, Prince, or foreign State.	**NO TITLES OR GIFTS** Congress will not give a Title, Such as a Prince, Earl, Duke or King. U.S. officers can't accept, From other countries, pay or things.

ARTICLE 1, Section 10, Clause 1

No State shall enter into any Treaty, Alliance, or Confederation; grant Letters of Marque and Reprisal; coin Money; emit Bills of Credit; make any Thing but gold and silver Coin a Tender in Payment of Debts; pass any Bill of Attainder, ex post facto Law, or Law impairing the Obligation of Contracts, or grant any Title of Nobility.

TREATIES, MONEY, OR BORDERS
States cannot make treaties,
With other countries, or allow,
Other countries to cross
Its borders, this does avow.
States also can't create
Their own money,
To pay for debts or things,
Obviously.

STANDARD MONEY
States can only accept standard money
To pay their debts, nor can States pass
Bills of Attainder (guilty without trial),
Or ex post facto Law, alas.

CONTRACTS OR TITLE OF NOBILITY
States can't pass laws that destroy,
Contracts that are in force,
And cannot give a title of
Nobility, of course.

MARQUE AND REPRISAL
Letters of Marque and Reprisal,
Found in Section Ten, not Six,
Means private boats cannot catch,
Or arrest enemy ships.

ARTICLE 1, Section 10, Clause 2

No State shall, without the Consent of the Congress, lay any Imposts or Duties on Imports or Exports, except what may be absolutely necessary for executing it's inspection Laws: and the net Produce of all Duties and Imposts, laid by any State on Imports or Exports, shall be for the Use of the Treasury of the United States; and all such Laws shall be subject to the Revision and Controul of the Congress.	<u>STATES TO BUY OR SELL</u> For States to buy or sell with other Countries, Congress must agree, And all the money that's collected, Goes to the U.S. Treasury.

ARTICLE 1, Section 10, Clause 3

No State shall, without the Consent of Congress, lay any Duty of Tonnage, keep Troops, or Ships of War in time of Peace, enter into any Agreement or Compact with another State, or with a foreign Power, or engage in War, unless actually invaded, or in such imminent Danger as will not admit of delay.	<u>ARMIES, WARSHIPS, AND WAR</u> Without consent from Congress, States can't keep any army troops, Or warships in times of peace, Or join forces with foreign groups. Without consent from Congress, States cannot go to war, unless, They're invaded and in danger, And in immediate distress.

ARTICLE 2

ARTICLE 2, Section 1, Clause 1

The executive Power shall be vested in a President of the United States of America. He shall hold his Office during the Term of four Years, and, together with the Vice President, chosen for the same Term, be elected, as follows	**LEADER OF THE U.S.** The leader of the U.S., Is the President, we affirm, Elected every four years, With the V.P. during that term.

ARTICLE 2, Section 1, Clause 2

Each State shall appoint, in such Manner as the Legislature thereof may direct, a Number of Electors, equal to the whole Number of Senators and Representatives to which the State may be entitled in the Congress: but no Senator or Representative, or Person holding an Office of Trust or Profit under the United States, shall be appointed an Elector. *Changed by the 12th Amendment*	**HOW MANY ELECTORS** The number of Representatives, And Senators of each state, Determine how many "ELECTORS" Each State has to vote – so great! **WHAT ARE ELECTORS?** "Electors" are people who Are selected to vote, For VP and President, As Article Two does quote. The Electoral College, Says that "electors" will choose, Who will win our elections, By voting, and who will lose. **CANNOT BE ELECTORS** Senators and Representatives, Cannot be Electors – No! Nor other government officers, Article Two says so.

ARTICLE 2, Section 1, Clause 3

*The **Electors shall meet in their respective States, and vote by Ballot** for two Persons, of whom one at least **shall not be an Inhabitant of the same State** with themselves. And they shall make a List of all the Persons voted for, and of the Number of Votes for each; which List they shall sign and certify, and transmit sealed to the Seat of the Government of the United States, directed to the President of the Senate.*

*The President of the Senate shall, in the Presence of the Senate and House of Representatives, **open all the Certificates, and the Votes shall then be counted.** The Person having the greatest Number of Votes shall be the President, if such Number be a Majority of the whole Number of Electors appointed; and if there be more than one who have such Majority, and have an equal Number of Votes, then the House of Representatives shall immediately chuse by Ballot one of them for President; and if no Person have a Majority, then from the five highest **on the List** the said House shall in like Manner chuse the President. But in chusing the President, the Votes shall be taken by States, the Representation from each State having one Vote; A quorum for this Purpose shall consist of a Member or Members from two thirds of the States, and a Majority of all the States shall be necessary to a Choice. In every Case, after the Choice of the President, the Person having the greatest Number of Votes of the Electors shall be the Vice President. But if there should remain two or more who have equal Votes, the Senate shall chuse from them by Ballot the Vice President. (Changed by the 12th Amendment)*

ELECTORS VOTE

Electors in their State's vote,
For two candidates,
By using written ballots,
That's how this translates.

FROM SAME STATE

At least one of the people,
Can't be from the same
State where that Elector lives,
Regardless of their name.

MAKE A LIST

The Electors make a list,
Who they all voted for,
And how many votes they got,
Signed and sealed for sure.
It then goes to the Congress,
To the President,
Of the U.S. Senate,
Addressed to be sent.

*The Electors shall meet in their respective States, and vote by Ballot for two Persons, of whom one at least shall not be an Inhabitant of the same State with themselves. And they shall **make a List of all the Persons voted for**, and of the Number of Votes for each; which **List they shall sign and certify**, and transmit sealed to the Seat of the Government of the United States, directed to the President of the Senate.*

*The President of the Senate shall, in the Presence of the Senate and House of Representatives, **open all the Certificates, and the Votes shall then be counted**. The Person having the greatest Number of Votes shall be the President, if such Number be a Majority of the whole Number of Electors appointed; and if there be more than one who have such Majority, **and have an equal Number of Votes**, then the House of Representatives shall immediately chuse by Ballot one of them for President; and if no Person have a Majority, then from the five highest on the List the said House shall in like Manner chuse the President. But in chusing the President, the Votes shall be taken by States, the Representation from each State having one Vote; A quorum for this Purpose shall consist of a Member or Members from two thirds of the States, and a Majority of all the States shall be necessary to a Choice. In every Case, after the Choice of the President, the Person having the greatest Number of Votes of the Electors shall be the Vice President. But if there should remain two or more who have equal Votes, the Senate shall chuse from them by Ballot the Vice President.*

Changed by the 12th Amendment

OPENS THE CERTIFICATES

The President of the Senate,
Opens the Certificates,
With votes from the Electors,
That were sent from all the States.
In front of all the Senators,
And Representatives too,
The votes are counted to announce
The winner, from this review.

MOST ELECTORAL VOTES

The person with the most
Electoral Votes wins,
And will be President,
When their term begins.
But if there is a tie,
Representatives choose.
One candidate will win;
The other one will lose.

DETAILS IN CLAUSE THREE

If there are complications,
With the majority,
While counting Electoral votes,
Read details in Clause Three.

ARTICLE 2, Section 1, Clause 4

The Congress may determine the Time of chusing the Electors, and the Day on which they shall give their Votes; which Day shall be the same throughout the United States.	**TIME AND DAY** Congress picks the time to choose, Electors, and the day, That they vote, on the same day, In all States, so they say.

ARTICLE 2, Section 1, Clause 5

*No Person except a **natural born Citizen**, or a Citizen of the United States, at the time of the Adoption of this Constitution, shall be eligible to the Office of President; neither shall any Person be eligible to that Office who shall not have attained to the **Age of thirty five Years**, and been **fourteen Years a Resident** within the United States.*	**TO BE PRESIDENT** To be President, you must be, Born in the U.S., we're told, Or a U.S. citizen, and, At least thirty-five years old. To be President, you must have, Lived in the United States, For at least fourteen years or more, So Article Two mandates.

ARTICLE 2, Section 1, Clause 6

In Case of the Removal of the President from Office, or of his **Death, Resignation, or Inability to discharge the Powers and Duties** of the said Office, the Same shall devolve on the **Vice President,** and the Congress may by Law provide for the Case of Removal, Death, Resignation or Inability, both of the President and Vice President, declaring what Officer shall then act as President, and such Officer shall act accordingly, until the Disability be removed, **or a President shall be elected.**

Amendment 25 changed this. House Speaker becomes President if both President and VP die.

IF THE PRESIDENT DIES

If the President dies, resigns,
Is removed, or cannot serve,
Then the Vice President's in charge,
For the Office to preserve.

IF PRESIDENT AND V.P.

If the President and V.P.,
Both leave, then Congress, instead,
Picks someone to hold office 'til,
A new President's elected.

ARTICLE 2, Section 1, Clause 7

The President shall, at stated Times, receive for his Services, **a Compensation**, which shall **neither be encreased nor diminished** during the Period for which he shall have been elected, and he shall not receive within that Period any other Emolument from the United States, or any of them.

PRESIDENT'S SALARY

The President gets a salary,
And while serving, it can't decrease.
They can't get paid other U.S. wages,
And their salary can't increase.

ARTICLE 2, Section 1, Clause 8

*Before he enter on the Execution of his Office, he shall take the following **Oath or Affirmation:**—"I do solemnly swear (or affirm) that I will faithfully execute the Office of President of the United States, and will to the best of my Ability, preserve, protect and defend the Constitution of the United States."*	**PRESIDENT'S OATH OF OFFICE** Before the President takes office, They make a solemn oath (affirm), To preserve, protect, and defend, The Constitution during their term. *"I promise most sincerely and truthfully that I will do my job as president of the United States, and I will, to the best of my ability, keep, protect and defend the Constitution of the United States."*

ARTICLE 2, Section 2, Clause 1

*The President shall be Commander in Chief of the **Army and Navy** of the United States, and of the Militia of the several States, when called into the actual Service of the United States; he may require the **Opinion, in writing**, of the principal Officer in each of the executive Departments, upon any Subject relating to the **Duties of their respective Offices**, and he shall have Power to grant Reprieves and Pardons for Offences against the United States, except in Cases of Impeachment.*	**NAVY AND ARMY** The President is in charge Of the Navy and Army, As the Commander-in-Chief, And other Military. The President is in charge Of the National Guard too, When called to serve the U.S., Protecting the red, white and blue. **IDEAS FROM OFFICERS** The President, may, in writing, Get ideas from Officers, About topics relating, To their duties or concerns.

ARTICLE 2, Section 2, Clause 1- CONTINUED

The President shall be Commander in Chief of the Army and Navy of the United States, and of the Militia of the several States, when called into the actual Service of the United States; *he may require the Opinion, in writing,* of the principal Officer in each of the executive Departments, upon any Subject relating to the Duties of their respective Offices, and he shall have **Power to grant Reprieves and Pardons** for Offences against the United States, except in Cases of Impeachment.

PARDON CRIMES
The President shall have power,
To pardon people for crimes,
Against the U.S., except for,
Impeachments, this clause defines.

ARTICLE 2, Section 2, Clause 2

He shall have Power, by and with the Advice and Consent of the Senate, **to make Treaties,** provided two thirds of the Senators present concur; and he shall nominate, and by and with the Advice and Consent of the Senate, shall **appoint Ambassadors,** other public Ministers and Consuls, Judges of the supreme Court, and all other Officers of the United States, whose Appointments are not herein otherwise provided for, and which shall be established by Law: but the Congress may by Law **vest the Appointment** of such inferior Officers, as they think proper, in the President alone, in the Courts of Law, or in the Heads of Departments.

MAKE TREATIES
The President can make treaties,
With other countries, although,
It must be approved by two-thirds,
Of Senators, you know?

AMBASSADORS
The President can appoint,
Ambassadors, with consent,
And U.S. Supreme Court Judges,
With advice from the Senate.

APPOINT OTHERS
Congress can let the President,
The Courts, or department heads,
Appoint other officers,
As they decide, it's said.

ARTICLE 2, Section 2, Clause 3

*The President shall have Power to **fill up all Vacancies** that may happen during the Recess of the Senate, by granting Commissions which shall expire at the End of their next Session.*

VACANCIES
When the Senate's not in session,
The U.S. President can fill,
Vacancies, until the end of
The next Senate session still.

ARTICLE 2, Section 3

*He shall from time to time give to the Congress Information of the **State of the Union**, and recommend to their Consideration such Measures as he shall judge necessary and expedient; he may, on extraordinary Occasions, convene both Houses, or either of them, and **in Case of Disagreement** between them, with Respect to the Time of Adjournment, he may adjourn them to such Time as he shall think proper; **he shall receive Ambassadors** and other public Ministers; he shall take Care that the Laws be faithfully executed, and shall Commission all the Officers of the United States.*

STATE OF THE UNION
The President, from time to time,
Gives Congress an update,
In a "State of the Union" speech,
With ideas to relate.

MEET ANYTIME
The President can meet with,
Congress when there's a need,
Also can stop the meeting,
Because they disagreed.

MEETS AND GREETS
The President meets and greets
Other countries' Ambassadors,
And makes sure that the laws are,
Enforced by U.S. Officers.

ARTICLE 2, Section 4

*The President, Vice President and all civil Officers of the United States, shall **be removed from Office** on Impeachment for, and Conviction of, Treason, Bribery, or other high Crimes and Misdemeanors.*	<u>REMOVED FROM OFFICE</u> The President, Vice President, Or Officer of the U.S., For Treason or for Bribery, Can be removed from their Office.

ARTICLE 3

ARTICLE 3, Section 1

*The judicial Power of the United States, shall be vested in one supreme Court, and in such inferior Courts as the Congress may from time to time ordain and establish. The Judges, both of the supreme and inferior Courts, **shall hold their Offices during good Behaviour**, and shall, at stated Times, receive for their Services, **a Compensation**, which shall not be diminished during their Continuance in Office.*

JUDICIAL POWER
All the Judicial Power,
Of the U.S. will be,
Headed by the Supreme Court,
We exclaim notably.

OTHER COURTS
Congress can set up other courts,
At times when there's a need,
And Supreme and lower Judges,
Can serve for life, indeed.

JUDGES SALARY
Judges will get a salary,
No, they don't work for free,
And their wages can't be lowered,
While they're a Judge, you see.

ARTICLE 3, Section 2, Clause 1

*The judicial Power shall extend to all **Cases, in Law and Equity, arising under this Constitution**, the Laws of the United States, and Treaties made, or which shall be made, under their Authority;—to all Cases affecting **Ambassadors, other public Ministers** and Consuls;—to all Cases of **admiralty and maritime Jurisdiction**;—to Controversies to which the United States shall be a Party;—to **Controversies between two or more States**;—between a State and Citizens of another State;—between Citizens of different States, —between Citizens of the same State claiming Lands under Grants of different States, and between a State, or the Citizens thereof, and foreign States, Citizens or Subjects.*

Part of this Clause was changed by Amendment 11

DECIDE CASES
The Judges of the courts have power,
To decide cases that involves,
Or questions the Constitution,
Its treaties, equity, and laws.

AMBASSADORS AND MINISTERS
Courts also decide cases,
About Ambassadors,
Who come from other countries,
And foreign ministers.

AT SEA
All cases of law about,
Ships and ports at sea,
Are decided by the Courts,
That's how it will be.

DISPUTES BETWEEN STATES
The Courts decide disputes between,
Two states or more, as well,
As between a State and country,
When things don't go so swell.

AMENDMENT 11 CHANGED THIS
This clause can be confusing,
How it is worded, so,
Amendment Eleven changed it,
To clarify, you know.

ARTICLE 3, Section 2, Clause 2

| In all Cases affecting **Ambassadors**, other public Ministers and Consuls, and those in which a State shall be Party, the **supreme Court shall have original Jurisdiction**. In all the other Cases before mentioned, the supreme Court shall have appellate Jurisdiction, both as to Law and Fact, with such Exceptions, and under such Regulations as the Congress shall make. | **AMBASSADOR CASES**
Cases of Ambassadors,
Consuls, Ministers too,
Go to the Supreme Court first,
For justice to pursue.

APPEAL
After cases have been heard,
Then they can appeal,
To the U.S. Supreme Court,
Yes, that is the deal!
 |

ARTICLE 3, Section 2, Clause 3

| The **Trial of all Crimes**, except in Cases of Impeachment, shall be by Jury; and such Trial shall be held in the State where the said Crimes shall have been committed; but when **not committed within any State**, the Trial shall be at such Place or Places as the Congress may by Law have directed. | **CRIMES TRIED BY JURY**
Trial for Federal crimes, except,
Impeachment will be by,
Jury, in the same State where,
The crime was, so don't cry.

PLACE FOR THE TRIAL
If a Federal crime is not,
Committed in a State,
The place for the trial will be,
Where Congress will dictate. |

ARTICLE 3, Section 3, Clause 1

*Treason against the United States, shall consist only in levying War against them, or in adhering to their Enemies, giving them Aid and Comfort. No Person shall be convicted of Treason unless on the **Testimony of two Witnesses** to the same overt Act, or on Confession in open Court.*	**TREASON IS** Treason is making war against, The U.S., or help out, An enemy of our country, A sad betrayal, no doubt. **TWO WITNESSES** No one can be found guilty, Of Treason unless there's two, Witnesses who see it, or, They confess to what they do.

ARTICLE 3, Section 3, Clause 2

*The Congress shall have Power to declare the **Punishment of Treason**, but no Attainder of Treason shall work Corruption of Blood, or Forfeiture except during the Life of the Person attainted.*	**PUNISH TREASON** The power to punish Treason, Is decided by the Congress. No family or other person, Can be punished for them, no less.

ARTICLE 4

ARTICLE 4, Section 1

*Full Faith and Credit shall be given in each State to the public Acts, Records, and judicial Proceedings of every other State. And the Congress may by general Laws prescribe the Manner in which such Acts, **Records** and Proceedings shall be proved, and the Effect thereof.*

RECORDS AND DECISIONS
Each state shall respect the laws,
Records, and court decisions,
Of all other States, of course,
With the proper precision.

WILL MAKE LAWS
Congress will make laws to decide,
How to check on each State's acts,
And if their records and reports,
Are effective, that's a fact!

ARTICLE 4, Section 2, Clause 1

The Citizens of each State shall be entitled to all Privileges and Immunities of Citizens in the several States.

CITIZENS OF EACH STATE
Citizens of each State,
Must each have all the same,
Rights and the protections,
As other States acclaim.

ARTICLE 4, Section 2, Clause 2

*A **Person charged** in any State with Treason, Felony, or other Crime, who shall flee from Justice, and be found in another State, shall on Demand of the executive Authority of the State from which he fled, **be delivered up**, to be removed to the State having Jurisdiction of the Crime.*	<u>CRIME IN ONE STATE</u> If someone charged with a crime, Runs to another State to flee, The Governor can demand, They return immediately.

ARTICLE 4, Section 2, Clause 3

*No Person held to Service or Labour in one State, under the Laws thereof, **escaping into another**, shall, in Consequence of any Law or Regulation therein, be discharged from such Service or Labour, but shall be delivered up on Claim of the Party to whom such Service or Labour may be due.* *Ended by Amendment 13 (slavery ended)*	<u>IF A SLAVE ESCAPES</u> If a slave escapes to a State where slaves are free, Then they must be returned to, Their owner, you see.

ARTICLE 4, Section 3, Clause 1

*New States may be admitted by the Congress into this Union; but **no new State shall be formed or erected within the Jurisdiction of any other State**; nor any State be formed by the Junction of two or more States, or Parts of States, without the Consent of the Legislatures of the States concerned as well as of the Congress.*	<u>STATES' JOIN SEPARATELY</u> One State can't join another, To create another State. States must join separately, For that is the mandate.

ARTICLE 4, Section 3, Clause 2

The Congress shall have Power to dispose of and make all needful **Rules and Regulations** *respecting the* **Territory or other Property belonging to the United States**; *and nothing in this Constitution shall be so construed as to Prejudice any Claims of the United States, or of any particular State.*	<u>RULES AND REGULATIONS</u> Congress shall have power to, Make all rules and regulation, For the lands and property, Belonging to this great nation.

ARTICLE 4, Section 4

The United States shall guarantee to every State in this Union a Republican Form of Government, and **shall protect each of them against Invasion;** *and on Application of the Legislature, or of the Executive (when the Legislature cannot be convened) against domestic Violence.*	<u>TO BE PROTECTED</u> A Republican form of Government, All the States are guaranteed, And against invasion and violence, They're to be protected, indeed.

ARTICLE 5

*The Congress, whenever **two thirds of both Houses shall deem it necessary, shall propose Amendments to this Constitution**, or, on the Application of the Legislatures of two thirds of the several States, shall call a **Convention for proposing Amendments,** which, in either Case, shall be valid to all Intents and Purposes, as Part of this Constitution, when ratified by the Legislatures of three fourths of the several States, or by Conventions in three fourths thereof, as the one or the other Mode of Ratification may be proposed by the Congress; Provided that no Amendment which may be made **prior to the Year One thousand eight hundred and eight** shall in any Manner affect the first and fourth Clauses in the Ninth section of the first article and that no State, without its Consent, shall be deprived of its equal Suffrage in the Senate.*

TWO-THIRDS
When two-thirds of both Houses,
Of the Congress see a need,
To change the Constitution,
It's Amendment time indeed!

CALL A CONVENTION
When two-thirds of Congress,
No more, or no less,
Proposes an amendment,
Off to each State it's sent.
States call a convention,
And if three fourths agree,
Then the Constitution,
Amended it will be.

YEAR EIGHTEEN-O-EIGHT
No Amendment can be made,
Before eighteen o-eight,
In Clauses One, Four, Section Nine,
Article One, oh great!
No state may lose its right to,
Equal number of votes,
In the Senate, affecting
The slave trade, yes we note.

ARTICLE 6

ARTICLE 6, Clause 1

All Debts contracted and Engagements entered into, before the Adoption of this Constitution, shall be as valid against the United States under this Constitution, as under the Confederation.	**BE PAID BACK** All the money that the U.S., Borrowed before the Constitution, Is required to be paid back, According to this resolution.

ARTICLE 6, Clause 2

*This Constitution, and the Laws of the United States which shall be made in Pursuance thereof; and all Treaties made, or which shall be made, under the Authority of the United States, shall be the **supreme Law of the Land**; and the **Judges** in every State shall be bound thereby, any Thing in the Constitution or Laws of any State to the Contrary notwithstanding.*	**SWEET LAND OF LIBERTY** The Constitution and the laws, And the treaties shall be, The Supreme Law of the land, Sweet land of liberty! **JUDGES JUDGE** How will judges judge? What will be their guide? The Constitution, Will help them decide.

ARTICLE 6, Clause 3

The Senators and Representatives before mentioned, and the Members of the several State Legislatures, and all executive and judicial Officers, both of the United States and of the several States, **shall be bound by Oath or Affirmation, to support this Constitution**; but **no religious Test** shall ever be required as a Qualification to any Office or public Trust under the United States.

OATH TO SUPPORT

Yes, by Oath or Affirmation,
U.S. Officers are bound,
To support the Constitution,
Because it's the best around!

NO RELIGIOUS TEST

Article Six makes it clear,
It is a law, not a request,
That for public office,
There can be no religious test.

ARTICLE 7

The Ratification of the Conventions of nine States, shall be sufficient for the Establishment of this Constitution between the States so ratifying the Same. Done in Convention **by the Unanimous Consent of the States present the Seventeenth Day of September in the Year of our Lord one thousand seven hundred and Eighty seven** *and of the Independence of the United States of America the Twelfth In witness whereof We have hereunto subscribed our Names,*

SEVENTEENTH OF SEPTEMBER
Seventeen eighty-seven,
Is a great year to remember!
The Constitution was signed,
On the seventeenth of September!

September 17th

UNANIMOUS CONSENT
Created in Convention,
By unanimous consent,
The Constitution is approved,
By the States that were present.

FINAL ARTICLE
Article Seven is the final,
Article, which makes it clear,
That our U.S. Constitution,
Is approved, so give a cheer!

SIGNERS OF THE U.S. CONSTITUTION

We sign our names as witnesses:

George WASHINGTON,
President and delegate from Virginia

Delaware
George Read
Gunning Bedford Jr.
John Dickinson
Richard Bassett
Jacob Broom

Maryland
James MCHenry
Dan of ST ThoS. Jenifer
Daniel Carroll

Virginia
John Blair
James Madison Jr.

North Carolina
William Blount, Hugh Williamson
Rich D. Dobbs Spaight

South Carolina
J. Rutledge
Charles I.A. Cotesworth Pinckney
Charles Pinckney
Pierce Butler

Georgia
William Few
Abraham Baldwin

New Hampshire
John Langdon
Nicholas Gilman

Massachusetts
Nathaniel Gorham
Rufus King

Connecticut
William Samuel Johnson
Roger Sherman

New York
Alexander Hamilton

New Jersey
William Livingston
David Brearley
William. Paterson
Jona: Dayton

Pennsylvania
B. Franklin
Thomas Mifflin
Robert T. Morris
George Clymer
Thomas. FitzSimons
Jared Ingersoll
James Wilson
Gouveneur Morris

Witness: William Jackson, Secretary

CHAPTER FOUR

Amendments to the Constitution (1-27)

BILL OF RIGHTS

Amendment 1: Individual Freedoms

Amendment 2: Right to Self-Defense

Amendment 3: Housing of Soldiers

Amendment 4: Privacy Rights

Amendment 5: Rights of Individuals in Criminal Cases

Amendment 6: Rights for a Fair Trial

Amendment 7: Rights in Civil Cases

Amendment 8: Bails, Fines, Punishments

Amendment 9: Rights Retained by the People

Amendment 10: Powers by the States and People

Amendment 11: Lawsuits Against States

Amendment 12: Election of President and Vice President

Amendment 13: Abolishment of Slavery

Amendment 14: Equal Protection

Amendment 15: Voting Rights

Amendment 16: Power to Tax

Amendment 17: Election of U.S. Senators

Amendment 18: Prohibition of Alcohol

Amendment 19: Women's Right to Vote

Amendment 20: Terms for President, VP, and Congress

Amendment 21: Repeal of Prohibition of Alcohol (#18)

Amendment 22: Limit of Presidential Terms

Amendment 23: Washington D.C. Voting

Amendment 24: Elimination of Voting Tax

Amendment 25: Succession of Office

Amendment 26: Eighteen-Year-Old Voter Right

Amendment 27: Congressional Pay Raises

AMENDMENTS

TWENTY-SEVEN AMENDMENTS
Our Constitution has,
Twenty-seven Amendments,
To protect our freedoms,
And our independence.

BILL OF RIGHTS
The rights of "We the People,"
The Constitution cites,
Are the first Ten Amendments,
Called the Bill of Rights!

DECEMBER 15, 1791
On December the fifteenth,
Seventeen ninety-one
The Bill of Rights was ratified,
A new day had begun!

BILL OF RIGHTS
Amendments 1-10
Ratified December 15, 1791

AMENDMENT 1
Individual Freedoms

*Congress shall make no law respecting an establishment of **religion**, or prohibiting the free exercise thereof; or abridging the **freedom of speech**, or of the **press;** or the right of the people **peaceably to assemble**, and to **petition** the Government for a redress of grievances.*

MAKE NO LAW
Freedom Of religion,
Of speech, and of the press,
Also to assemble,
And petition for redress.
Congress shall make no law,
Against none of these things,
For "We, the people", and,
The freedom that it brings.

FIVE RIGHTS
The five rights that protect us,
Are found in Amendment One:
Freedom of Religion, Speech,
Press, Assemble, Petition.

TO PETITION
When we see that's
something's wrong,
We can tell the government.
To Petition is our right,
Without fear of punishment.

AMENDMENT 2
Rights to Self-Defense

Right to Bear Arms *A well regulated Militia, being necessary to the security of a free State, the right of the people to keep and bear Arms, shall not be infringed.* 	<u>BEAR ARMS</u> The right to bear arms, To own guns cannot be, Infringed upon, To preserve liberty. <u>PROTECT OURSELVES</u> Our right to protect, Ourselves and others must be, Always protected, In this land of the free.

AMENDMENT 3
Housing of Soldiers

Quartering of Soldiers *No Soldier shall, in time of peace be quartered in any house, without the consent of the Owner, nor in time of war, but in a manner to be prescribed by law.* 	<u>SOLDIERS CAN'T STAY</u> Soldiers cannot reside, In your home to stay, Whether in peace or war, Unless the owners say. <u>TIME OF WAR</u> If in time of war, Soldiers come to stay, Unless a law is passed, They must go away.

AMENDMENT 4
Privacy Rights

Search and Seizure

The right of the people to be secure in their persons, houses, papers, and effects, against **unreasonable searches and seizures**, *shall not be violated, and no Warrants shall issue, but upon probable cause, supported by Oath or affirmation, and particularly describing the place to be searched, and the persons or things to be seized.*

SEARCH OR SEIZE
My home or my property,
Or even myself,
Cannot be searched or removed,
From my house or shelf.
Without a warrant from a judge,
No one can search or seize,
And by law, must have good cause,
Amendment Four agrees!

GOOD REASON
If there is a good reason,
To search or take property,
By Oath, they must describe,
What to take and what to see.

PROPERTY RIGHTS
Without Property Rights,
We have no rights at all.
Stand for Property Rights,
To not let freedom fall!

AMENDMENT 5
Rights for Individuals in Criminal Cases

Criminal Cases / Private Property

No person shall be held to answer for a capital, or otherwise infamous crime, unless on a presentment or indictment of a Grand Jury, except in cases arising in the land or naval forces, or in the Militia, when in actual service in time of War or public danger; nor shall any person be subject for the same offense to be twice put in jeopardy of life or limb; nor shall be compelled in any criminal case to be a witness against himself, nor be deprived of life, liberty, or property, without due process of law; nor shall private property be taken for public use, without just compensation.

PUT ON TRIAL
A person can't be put on trial,
For a serious crime,
Unless a grand jury says so,
In peace or war time.

CHARGED TWICE
A person can't be charged,
For the same crime twice.
That's "Double Jeopardy,"
And it isn't nice.

SELF-INCRIMINATION
A citizen can't be forced,
To say that they're guilty.
That's self-incrimination,
So they don't have to plea.

LIFE, LIBERTY OR PROPERTY
Life, liberty or property,
The Government can't take,
Without due-process of law,
For rights and freedom's sake.

PUBLIC USE
Your private property,
Cannot be taken away,
For any public use,
Without giving you fair pay.

AMENDMENT 6
Rights for a Fair Trial

Fair Trial

*In all criminal prosecutions, the accused shall enjoy **the right to a speedy and public trial**, by an impartial jury of the State and district wherein the crime shall have been committed, which district shall have been previously ascertained by law, and to **be informed of the nature and cause of the accusation**; to be confronted with the witnesses against him; to have compulsory process for **obtaining witnesses in his favor,** and to have the Assistance of Counsel for his defence.*

FAIR, PUBLIC TRIAL
A person has a right,
To a fair, public trial,
In the same place the crime,
Happened, all the while.

TOLD WHY
If you're accused of a crime,
You must be told why,
And can face your accuser,
To look them in the eye.

WITNESS AND COUNSEL
An accused has the right,
To have a witness,
And to have some Counsel,
Come to their defense.

AMENDMENT 7
Rights in Civil Cases

Right to a Jury

In Suits at common law, where the value in controversy shall exceed twenty dollars, the right of trial by jury shall be preserved, and no fact tried by a jury, shall be otherwise re-examined in any Court of the United States, than according to the rules of the common law.

CIVIL CASES
Amendment Seven makes it clear,
Civil cases can be heard.
Amendment Seven gives the right,
To a jury, it's assured.

JURIES
Juries are for,
Civil cases too,
Not just criminal,
Oh yes, it is true!

RIGHT TO A JURY
A right to a jury,
Of common law, you see,
For some civil cases,
Helps maintain liberty.

AMENDMENT 8
Bails, Fines, Punishments

Excessive Bail /
Cruel and Unusual Punishment

Excessive bail shall not be required, nor excessive fines imposed, nor cruel and unusual punishments inflicted.

CRUEL PUNISHMENT
Cruel and Unusual,
Punishment, when charged
with a crime,
Cannot be inflicted,
On anyone at any time.

EXCESSIVE FINES OR BAIL
Amendment eight states,
Fines or bail can't be,
Excessively high,
And no cruelty.

AMENDMENT 9
Rights Retained by the People

Construction of Constitution The enumeration in the Constitution, of certain rights, shall not be construed to deny or disparage others retained by the people. 	<u>RIGHTS NOT LISTED</u> Some rights aren't listed, In the Constitution, But there is no way, To spell out every one. Rights that aren't listed, Must not be denied, Rights must be protected, That are not described. <u>ENUMERATION OF</u> The enumeration, Every right one by one, That is not listed, In the Constitution, Belongs to the people, Not to the government, This protects our rights, That's the message that's sent!

AMENDMENT 10
Powers by the States and People

The powers not delegated to the United States by the Constitution, nor prohibited by it to the States, are reserved to the States respectively, or to the people.	<u>STATES OR PEOPLE</u> Powers that the Constitution, Does not give to the U.S., Belongs to the States or people, To be free and to progress.

AMENDMENT 11
Lawsuits Against States – Ratified February 7, 1795

The Judicial power of the United States shall not be construed to extend to any suit in law or equity, commenced or prosecuted against one of the United States by Citizens of another State, or by Citizens or Subjects of any Foreign State.

BETWEEN STATES
If one State wants to sue another,
Federal courts can't get involved,
Nor between another country.
By the States it is resolved.

FEBRUARY 7, 1795
On February seventh,
Seventeen ninety-five,
Amendment Eleven,
Was approved and ratified.

CHANGED ARTICLE THREE
Amendment Eleven changed,
Article Three, Section Two,
How States sue other States,
And what the courts can't do.

AMENDMENT 12
Election of President and Vice President – Ratified June 15, 1804

Choosing the President and Vice President

The Electors **shall meet in their respective states, and vote** *by ballot for President and Vice President, one of whom, at least,* **shall not be an inhabitant of the same state** *with themselves; they shall name in their ballots the person voted for as President, and in distinct ballots the person voted for as Vice-President, and they shall make distinct lists of all persons voted for as President, and of all persons voted for as Vice-President and of the number of votes for each, which lists they shall sign and certify, and transmit sealed to the seat of the government of the United States, directed to the President of the Senate;*

The President of the Senate shall, in the presence of the Senate and House of Representatives, open all the certificates and the votes shall then be counted;

The person having the greatest Number of votes for President, **shall be the President, if such number be a majority of the whole number of Electors appointed**; *and if no person have such majority, then from the persons having the highest numbers not exceeding three on the list of those voted for as President, the House of Representatives shall choose immediately, by ballot, the President.*

ELECTIONS
The President and Vice President,
Follow rules to be elected.
Amendment Twelve changed
the system,
For them to be selected.

ELECTORS WILL MEET
Electors in each State will meet,
In their own States and vote,
By ballot for President,
And Vice President, we note.

FROM THE SAME STATE
Candidates for the President,
And Vice President can't be,
From the same State, and Electors,
Will vote for them separately.

MOST VOTES
The candidate with the most votes,
Wins the Presidency,
As long as the new President,
Has the majority.

Election of President and Vice President – Ratified June 15, 1804

But in choosing the President, the votes shall be taken by states, the representation from each state having one vote; **a quorum for this purpose shall consist of a member or members from two-thirds of the states,** *and a majority of all the states shall be necessary to a choice. And if the House of Representatives shall not choose a President whenever the right of choice shall devolve upon them,* **before the fourth day of March** *next following, then the Vice-President shall act as President, as in the case of the death or other constitutional disability of the President.*

The person having the greatest number of votes as Vice-President, shall be the Vice-President, *if such number be a majority of the whole number of Electors appointed, and if no person have a majority, then from the two highest numbers on the list, the Senate shall choose the Vice-President; a quorum for the purpose shall consist of two-thirds of the whole number of Senators, and a majority of the whole number shall be necessary to a choice.* **But no person constitutionally ineligible to the office of President shall be eligible to that of Vice-President** *of the United States.*

The 20th Amendment added more on this topic

NO MAJORITY
If no candidate gets a majority,
Then the House must cast their vote,
For one of the top, three Presidential,
Candidates, who they denote.

A QUORUM
Each of the Representatives,
Has one vote from each State,
A Quorum will be at least one
Member from two-thirds, great!

BY MARCH FOURTH
A majority of all
The States must then consent,
By March Fourth or the VP
Will become President.

MOST VOTES
The V.P. with the most votes,
Shall be Vice-President,
As long as the new VP,
Has the highest percent.

REQUIREMENTS
The guidelines to be President,
And VP are the same.
They must meet the requirements,
Amendment Twelve does claim.

AMENDMENT 13
Abolishment of Slavery – Ratified December 6, 1865

Slavery Abolished

1. *Neither slavery nor involuntary servitude, except as a punishment for crime whereof the party shall have been duly convicted, shall exist within the United States, or any place subject to their jurisdiction.*

2. *Congress shall have power to enforce this article by appropriate legislation.*

NO SLAVERY
On January thirty-first,
Of eighteen sixty-five,
At last the end of slavery,
Had finally arrived!

LAWS TO ENFORCE
Congress will have power,
To make laws that they need,
For Amendment Thirteen,
Now that the slaves are freed.

AMENDMENT 14, Section 1
Equal Protection – Ratified July 9, 1868

Citizens Rights

1. **All persons born or naturalized in the United States,** *and subject to the jurisdiction thereof, are citizens of the United States and of the State wherein they reside.* **No State shall make or enforce any law which shall abridge the privileges or immunities of citizens** *of the United States; nor shall any State* **deprive any person of life, liberty, or property, without due process of law***; nor deny to any person within its jurisdiction the equal protection of the laws.*

U.S. CITIZENSHIP
Anyone born in the United States,
Or by naturalization,
Are citizens of the State,
where they live,
And citizens of this nation.

LIMIT OR LESSON RIGHTS
States cannot make or enforce,
Any laws that limit rights,
Privileges, or Protections,
Of citizens, this cites.

EQUAL PROTECTION
Life, liberty, or property,
Cannot be taken away,
By the States without due process,
To keep tyranny at bay.

AMENDMENT 14, Section 2
Equal Protection – Ratified July 9, 1868

Citizens Rights

*2. Representatives shall be apportioned among the several States **according to their respective numbers,** counting the whole number of persons in each State, **excluding Indians not taxed.** But when the right to vote at any election for the choice of electors for President and Vice President of the United States, Representatives in Congress, the Executive and Judicial officers of a State, or the members of the Legislature thereof, is denied to any of the male inhabitants of such State, being twenty-one years of age, and citizens of the United States, or in any way abridged, except for participation in rebellion, or other crime, **the basis of representation therein shall be reduced in the proportion which the number of such male citizens shall bear to the whole number of male citizens twenty-one years of age** in such State.*

NUMBER OF PEOPLE
The number of Representatives,
In the House, to make things fair,
Is based on how many people,
In each State is living there.
Native Americas, in fact,
Are not counted,
since they're not taxed.

MALES OVER TWENTY-ONE
If a State doesn't let a male
Citizen, over twenty-one,
Vote, then Representatives,
Will be reduced, and that's no fun.

AMENDMENT 14, Section 3
Equal Protection – Ratified July 9, 1868

Citizens Rights

3. *No person shall be a Senator or Representative in Congress, or elector of President and Vice President, or hold any office, civil or military, under the United States, or under any State, who,* **having previously taken an oath,** *as a member of Congress, or as an officer of the United States, or as a member of any State legislature, or as an executive or judicial officer of any State, to support the Constitution of the United States,* **shall have engaged in insurrection or rebellion against the same, or given aid or comfort to the enemies thereof.** *But Congress may by a vote of two thirds of each House, remove such disability.*

JOINING THE ENEMY
Before the Civil War,
There were some who had,
Taken an Oath of office,
But then things went bad.
Some of them broke their oath,
And they did rebel,
Joining the enemy,
Which didn't turn out so well.

CONFEDERATE OFFICER
A Confederate Officer,
Who rebelled in the Civil War,
Without Congress' two-thirds vote,
Can't serve in Congress any more.

AMENDMENT 14, Section 4 & 5
Equal Protection – Ratified July 9, 1868

Citizens Rights

*4. The validity of the **public debt** of the United States, authorized by law, including debts incurred for payment of pensions and bounties for services in suppressing insurrection or rebellion, shall not be questioned. But neither the United States nor any State **shall assume or pay any debt or obligation incurred in aid of insurrection or rebellion against the United States, or any claim for the loss or emancipation of any slave;** but all such debts, obligations and claims shall be held illegal and void.*

*5. The Congress shall have power **to enforce**, by appropriate legislation, the provisions of this article.*

PAID BACK
Any money that the United States,
Spent during the Civil War,
To fight against the Confederacy,
Will get paid back for sure.
But debts by the Confederacy,
From their battles and attacks,
Including claims of freeing slaves,
Is void, and won't get paid back.

THIS AMENDMENT
The Congress can make laws,
Laws that will enforce,
This Fourteenth Amendment,
That has been endorsed.

AMENDMENT 15, Section 1 & 2
Voting Rights – Ratified February 3, 1870

Voting Rights

1. The right of citizens of the United States to vote shall not be denied or abridged by the United States or by any State on account of race, color, or previous condition of servitude.

2. The Congress shall have power to enforce this article by appropriate legislation.

RACE OR COLOR
No citizen can be denied,
The right to vote, anymore,
Because of their race, color,
Or if they were a slave before.

BY LAW
Congress has the power,
By law to enforce,
This Fifteenth Amendment,
Yes they do, of course.

AMENDMENT 16
Power to Tax – Ratified February 3, 1913

Power to Tax

The Congress shall have power to lay and collect taxes on incomes, from whatever source derived, without apportionment among the several States, and without regard to any census or enumeration.

POWER TO TAX
Congress has power to tax,
All Citizens' income,
Regardless of what State,
The citizen is from.

AMENDMENT 17
Election of U.S. Senators – Ratified April 8, 1913

Senators Elected by Popular Vote

*The Senate of the United States shall be composed of **two Senators from each State, elected by the people thereof, for six years; and each Senator shall have one vote.** The electors in each State shall have **the qualifications** requisite for electors of the most numerous branch of the State legislatures. **When vacancies happen** in the representation of any State in the Senate, the executive authority of such State shall issue writs of election to fill such vacancies: Provided, That the legislature of any State may empower the executive thereof to make temporary appointments until the people fill the vacancies by election as the legislature may direct. This amendment shall not be so construed as to affect the election or term of **any Senator chosen before it becomes valid as part of the Constitution.***

PEOPLE VOTE
The people, not State Legislatures,
Were given the voting right,
To elect their U.S. Senators,
With the proper oversight.

TWO SENATORS
The Senate of the U.S.,
Has two Senators from each State,
Elected by the People,
Every six years, with one vote, mate.

QUALIFICATIONS
Elector's qualifications,
Must all be the same, for sure,
As Electors of the biggest
House of State Legislature.

SENATOR VACANCY
If a Senator leaves office,
And there is a vacancy,
The Governor can then appoint,
Someone temporarily.

CHOSEN BEFORE
This Amendment doesn't affect
The term of any Senator,
Who was chosen before it was
Ratified, and that is for sure.

AMENDMENT 18, Section 1
Prohibition of Alcohol – Ratified January 16, 1919

Liquor Abolished *1. After one year from the ratification of this article the manufacture, sale, or transportation of intoxicating liquors within, the importation thereof into, or the exportation thereof from the United States and all territory subject to the jurisdiction thereof for beverage purposes is hereby prohibited.*	**PROHIBITION** In the year nineteen-nineteen, A ratification, Stopped the sale of alcohol, Known as Prohibition. **BEER OR WINE** No more selling or transporting, Beer, liquor, or wine, One year after this Amendment, That is the deadline.

AMENDMENT 18, Section 2
Prohibition of Alcohol – Ratified January 16, 1919

2. The Congress and the several States shall have concurrent power to enforce this article by appropriate legislation.	**TO ENFORCE** Both the Congress and the States, Have power to make laws, To enforce this Amendment, But no need for applause.

AMENDMENT 18, Section 3
Prohibition of Alcohol – Ratified January 16, 1919

3. This article shall be inoperative unless it shall have been ratified as an amendment to the Constitution by the legislatures of the several States, as provided in the Constitution, within seven years from the date of the submission hereof to the States by the Congress.	**WITHIN SEVEN YEARS** For the Eighteen Amendment, To be put into effect, It must be ratified by, Seven years, that's correct.

AMENDMENT 18
Prohibition of Alcohol – Ratified January 16, 1919

REPEALED – Amendment XVIII (18)
Oh, the Eighteenth Amendment,
To prohibit alcohol,
Was repealed by Amendment
Twenty-one, once and for all.

1919-1933 – Amendment XVIII (18)
From nineteen-nineteen,
'Til nineteen thirty-three,
Alcohol was banned,
By Congress legally.

AMENDMENT 19
Women's Right to Vote – Ratified August 18, 1920

Women's Suffrage

*The right of citizens of the United States to vote **shall not be denied** or abridged by the United States or by any State on account of sex. Congress shall have power to enforce this article by appropriate legislation.*

WOMENS RIGHT TO VOTE
Women have the right to vote,
It cannot be denied.
Congress can enforce this law,
To make sure it's applied.

1920
Women got the right to vote,
Such a sight to see!
Amendment Nineteen happened,
In Nineteen twenty.

AMENDMENT 20, Section 1
Terms for President, VP, and Congress – Ratified January 23, 1933

Presidential, Congressional Terms

*1. The terms of the President and Vice President shall **end at noon on the 20th day of January**, and the terms of Senators and Representatives at noon on the 3rd day of January, of the years in which such terms would have ended if this article had not been ratified; and the terms of their successors shall then begin.*

TERM ENDS
On January twentieth,
The President's term ends,
And so does the Vice President's,
But they can still be friends.

AMENDMENT 20, Section 2
Terms for President, VP, and Congress – Ratified January 23, 1933

2. The Congress shall assemble at least once in every year, and such meeting shall begin at **noon on the 3d day of January,** *unless they shall by law appoint a different day.*	<u>JANUARY THIRD</u> Congress meets at least once a year, On January third, Unless they choose a different day, If it is preferred.

AMENDMENT 20, Section 3
Terms for President, VP, and Congress – Ratified January 23, 1933

3. If, at the time fixed for the beginning of the term of the President, the President elect shall have died, the Vice President elect shall become President. **If a President shall not have been chosen before the time fixed for the beginning of his term,** *or if the President elect shall have failed to qualify, then the Vice President elect shall act as President* **until a President shall have qualified;** *and the* **Congress may by law provide for the case wherein neither a President elect nor a Vice President elect shall have qualified,** *declaring who shall then act as President, or the manner in which one who is to act shall be selected, and such person shall act accordingly until a President or Vice President shall have qualified.*	<u>BY JANUARY TWENTIETH</u> If by January twentieth, No President's been chosen, Or, if the elected President, Based on the Constitution, Is not qualified to serve, then, The Vice President will act, As President until one is, Chosen, and that's a fact. <u>IF NEITHER QUALIFY</u> If neither the President-Elect, Nor VP-Elect aren't qualified, Then who acts as the President, Or how to choose, Congress decides.

AMENDMENT 20, Section 4
Terms for President, VP, and Congress – Ratified January 23, 1933

4. The Congress may by law provide for the case of the death of any of the persons from whom the House of Representatives may choose a President whenever the right of choice shall have devolved upon them, and **for the case of the death** of any of the persons from whom the Senate may choose a Vice President whenever the right of choice shall have devolved upon them.	**VP OR PRESIDENT** Laws will be made by Congress, If the President or VP, Dies before taking Office, In such a time of tragedy.

AMENDMENT 20, Section 5
Terms for President, VP, and Congress – Ratified January 23, 1933

5. Sections 1 and 2 shall take effect on the 15th day of October following the ratification of this article	**SECTION ONE AND TWO** Section One and Two, Will both be effective on, October fifteenth, After Ratification.

AMENDMENT 20, Section 6
Terms for President, VP, and Congress – Ratified January 23, 1933

6. This article shall be inoperative unless it shall have been ratified as an amendment to the Constitution by the legislatures of **three-fourths of the several States within seven years** from the date of its submission.	**SEVEN YEARS** This Amendment will not be, Effective unless approved, For the Constitution by, Legislatures, that include: Three-fourths of the several States, Within up to seven years, From the date of submission, This Section so appears.

AMENDMENT 21, Section 1 & 2
Repeal of Prohibition of Alcohol – Ratified December 5, 1933

Amendment 18 Repealed *1. The eighteenth article of amendment to the Constitution of the United States is hereby repealed.* *2. The transportation or importation into any State, Territory, or possession of the United States for delivery or use therein of intoxicating liquors, in violation of the laws thereof, is hereby prohibited.*	<u>ALCOHOL IS LEGAL</u> Alcohol is legal again, Amendment Eighteen, thrown out. Each State can make their own laws, About alcohol, no doubt.

AMENDMENT 21, Section 3
Repeal of Prohibition of Alcohol – Ratified December 5, 1933

3. The article shall be inoperative unless it shall have been ratified as an amendment to the Constitution by conventions in the several States, as provided in the Constitution, within seven years from the date of the submission hereof to the States by the Congress.	<u>TO BE VERIFIED</u> Amendment Twenty-one, Must be ratified, Within seven years, To be verified.

AMENDMENT 22, Section 1
Limit of Presidential Terms – Ratified February 27, 1951

Presidential Term Limits

1. No person shall be elected to the office of the President more than twice, and no person who has held the office of President, or acted as President, for more than two years of a term to which some other person was elected President shall be elected to the office of the President more than once. But this Article shall not apply to any person holding the office of President, when this Article was proposed by the Congress, and shall not prevent any person who may be holding the office of President, or acting as President, during the term within which this Article becomes operative from holding the office of President or acting as President during the remainder of such term.

TWO-YEAR TERM
The President cannot serve,
More than a two-year term,
Says Amendment Twenty-two,
Which clearly does confirm.

DOESN'T APPLY
This Amendment doesn't apply,
To the President right now,
Not until this Amendment is,
Officially approved, wow!

AMENDMENT 22, Section 2
Limit of Presidential Terms – Ratified February 27, 1951

2. This article shall be inoperative unless it shall have been ratified as an amendment to the Constitution by the legislatures of three-fourths of the several States within seven years from the date of its submission to the States by the Congress.

TAKE EFFECT
This Amendment will take effect,
Within seven years from the day,
It was submitted to the States,
Then everything will be okay.

AMENDMENT 23, Section 1
Washington D.C. Voting – Ratified March 29, 1961

The District

*1. **The District** constituting the seat of Government of the United States shall appoint in such manner as the Congress may direct: **A number of electors** of President and Vice President equal to the whole number of Senators and Representatives in Congress to which the District would be entitled **if it were a State**, but in no event more than **the least populous State; they shall be in addition to those appointed by the States**, but they shall be considered, for the purposes of the election of President and Vice President, to be electors appointed by a State; and they shall meet in the District and perform such duties as provided by the **twelfth article of amendment**.*

DISTRICT OF COLUMBIA
The District of Columbia,
(Now called Washington D.C.),
Can vote for the President,
By electors, yes sirree!

AS IF A STATE
The number of Electors is,
Figured as if they were a State,
And shouldn't be more Electors than,
The smallest State, possibly great.

ELECTORS IN ADDITION
These Electors are in addition,
To Electors from those States,
To elect VP and President,
This Amendment demonstrates.

MEET AND VOTE
The District Electors,
Of Columbia will meet,
And vote as in the Twelfth,
Amendment, isn't that sweet?

AMENDMENT 23, Section 2
Washington D.C. Voting – Ratified March 29, 1961

The District 2. The Congress shall have power to enforce this article by appropriate legislation.	**ENFORCEABLE** Congress has the power, To enforce this Article, How? By legislation, That's how it's enforceable.

AMENDMENT 24, Section 1
Elimination of Voting Tax – Ratified January 23, 1964

Voting Tax 1. The right of citizens of the United States to vote in any primary or other election for President or Vice President, for electors for President or Vice President, or for Senator or Representative in Congress, shall not be denied or abridged by the United States or any State by reason of failure to pay any poll tax or other tax. 	**VOTING TAX** A citizen cannot be made, To pay a voting tax, Or take a reading test to vote, So you can just relax!

AMENDMENT 24, Section 2
Elimination of Voting Tax – Ratified January 23, 1964

2. The Congress shall have power to enforce this article by appropriate legislation.	**BE UPHELD** And by law the Congress has, Power to enforce , This Amendment so it will, Be upheld, of course.

AMENDMENT 25, Section 1
Succession of Office – Ratified February 10, 1967

Succession of Office *1. In case of the removal of the President from office or of his death or resignation, the Vice President shall become President.*	**DIES OR REMOVED** If the President dies, or is, Removed, or resigns, The VP becomes President, As per the guidelines.

AMENDMENT 25, Section 2
Succession of Office – Ratified February 10, 1967

2. Whenever there is a vacancy in the office of the Vice President, the President shall nominate a Vice President who shall take office upon confirmation by a majority vote of both Houses of Congress.	**IF VP DIES OR RESIGNS** If VP dies, resigns, removed, The President will choose, Another, but both Houses of The Congress must approve.

AMENDMENT 25, Section 3
Succession of Office – Ratified February 10, 1967

*3. Whenever the President transmits to the President pro tempore of the Senate and the Speaker of the House of Representatives his written declaration that **he is unable to discharge the powers and duties of his office**, and until he transmits to them a **written declaration** to the contrary, such powers and duties shall be discharged by the Vice President as Acting President.*	**CAN'T DO THE JOB** If the President can't do the job, That they are supposed to do, They tell the Senate and the Speaker, In a letter, yes it's true. Then the Vice President becomes, The Acting President, Until the President returns, And another letter's sent.

AMENDMENT 25, Section 4
Succession of Office – Ratified February 10, 1967

*4. Whenever the Vice President and a majority of either the principal officers of the executive departments or of such other body as Congress may by law provide, transmit to the President pro tempore of the Senate and the Speaker of the House of Representatives their **written declaration that the President is unable to discharge the powers and duties of his office,** the Vice President shall **immediately assume the powers** and duties of the office as Acting President.*

*Thereafter, when the President transmits to the President pro tempore of the Senate and the Speaker of the House of Representatives his **written declaration** that no inability exists, he shall resume the powers and duties of his office unless the Vice President and a majority of either the principal officers of the executive department or of such other body as Congress may by law provide, **transmit within four days** to the President pro tempore of the Senate and the Speaker of the House of Representatives their written declaration that the President is unable to discharge the powers and duties of his office. Thereupon **Congress shall decide the issue, assembling within forty eight hours** for that purpose if not in session. If the Congress, **within twenty one days** after receipt of the latter written declaration, or, if Congress is not in session, within twenty one days after Congress is required to assemble, determines by two thirds vote of both Houses that the President is unable to discharge the powers and duties of his office, **the Vice President shall continue to discharge the same as Acting President;** otherwise, the President shall resume the powers and duties of his office.*

IF THE PRESIDENT
If the President can't write,
The letter, the VP can,
With Cabinet majority,
Of the unexpected plan.
The VP becomes Acting,
President until the day,
When the President returns,
Prepared to lead the way.

WITHIN FOUR DAYS
The Vice President and others,
Must send a letter to declare,
Within four days, the President,
Can't work, so they're aware.

WITHIN FORTY-EIGHT HOURS
If all of these things happen,
Congress gathers to meet,
Within forty-eight hours,
This issue to entreat.

TWENTY-ONE DAYS
Congress has twenty-one days,
To decide, by a two-thirds vote.
If the President can't work,
The VP will keep things afloat.

AMENDMENT 26, Section 1
Eighteen-Year-Old Voter Right – Ratified July 1, 1971

Voter Rights for Eighteen-Year-Olds *1. The right of citizens of the United States, who are eighteen years of age or older, to vote shall not be denied or abridged by the United States or by any State on account of age.* 	<u>EIGHTEEN YEARS OLD</u> A U.S. citizen can vote, If they're eighteen years old, No one can take that right away, By Congress we are told!

AMENDMENT 26, Section 2
Eighteen-Year-Old Voter Right – Ratified July 1, 1971

2. The Congress shall have power to enforce this article by appropriate legislation.	<u>ENFORCED</u> Amendment Twenty-Six, By law can be enforced, To protect citizens, Approved and endorsed.

AMENDMENT 27
Congressional Pay Raises – Ratified July 1, 1971

Limiting Changes to Congressional Pay *No law, varying the compensation for the services of the Senators and Representatives, shall take effect, until an election of Representatives shall have intervened.*	<u>CONGRESSIONAL PAY RAISE</u> Congress cannot get a raise, 'Til after the next election. Their new salary must wait, Even if there's an objection.

CHAPTER FIVE

Resources

Preamble to the U.S. Constitution

Signers of the U.S. Constitution

Declaration of Independence

Signers of the Declaration of Independence

Presidents of the United States

Pledge of Allegiance

PREAMBLE TO THE
U.S. CONSTITUTION

*"We the People of the United States,
in Order to form a more perfect Union,
establish Justice,
insure domestic Tranquility,
provide for the common defense,
promote the general Welfare,
and secure the Blessings of Liberty
to ourselves and our Posterity,
do ordain and establish this Constitution
for the United States of America."*

SIGNERS OF THE U.S. CONSTITUTION

We sign our names as witnesses:

George WASHINGTON,
President and delegate from Virginia

Delaware
George Read
Gunning Bedford Jr.
John Dickinson
Richard Bassett
Jacob Broom

Maryland
James MCHenry
Dan of ST ThoS. Jenifer
Daniel Carroll

Virginia
John Blair
James Madison Jr.

North Carolina
William Blount, Hugh Williamson
Rich D. Dobbs Spaight

South Carolina
J. Rutledge
Charles I.A. Cotesworth Pinckney
Charles Pinckney
Pierce Butler

Georgia
William Few
Abraham Baldwin

New Hampshire
John Langdon
Nicholas Gilman

Massachusetts
Nathaniel Gorham
Rufus King

Connecticut
William Samuel Johnson
Roger Sherman

New York
Alexander Hamilton

New Jersey
William Livingston
David Brearley
William. Paterson
Jona: Dayton

Pennsylvania
B. Franklin
Thomas Mifflin
Robert T. Morris
George Clymer
Thomas. FitzSimons
Jared Ingersoll
James Wilson
Gouveneur Morris

Witness: William Jackson, Secretary

DECLARATION OF INDEPENDENCE

IN CONGRESS, July 4, 1776.
The unanimous Declaration of
The thirteen united States of America,

When in the Course of human events, it becomes necessary for one people to dissolve the political bands which have connected them with another, and to assume among the powers of the earth, the separate and equal station to which the Laws of Nature and of Nature's God entitle them, a decent respect to the opinions of mankind requires that they should declare the causes which impel them to the separation.

We hold these truths to be self-evident, that all men are created equal, that they are endowed by their Creator with certain unalienable Rights, that among these are Life, Liberty and the pursuit of Happiness.–That to secure these rights, Governments are instituted among Men, deriving their just powers from the consent of the governed,

–That whenever any Form of Government becomes destructive of these ends, it is the Right of the People to alter or to abolish it, and to institute new Government, laying its foundation on such principles and organizing its powers in such form, as to them shall seem most likely to effect their Safety and Happiness. Prudence, indeed, will dictate that Governments long established should not be changed for light and transient causes; and accordingly all experience hath shewn, that mankind are more disposed to suffer, while evils are sufferable, than to right themselves by abolishing the forms to which they are accustomed. But when a long train of abuses and usurpations, pursuing invariably the same Object evinces a design to reduce them under absolute Despotism, it is their right, it is their duty, to throw off such Government, and to provide new Guards for their future security.–Such has been the patient sufferance of these Colonies; and such is now the necessity   which constrains them to alter their former Systems of Government. The history of the present King of Great Britain is a history of repeated injuries and usurpations, all having in direct object the establishment of an absolute Tyranny over these States. To prove this, let Facts be submitted to a candid world.

He has refused his Assent to Laws, the most wholesome and necessary for the public good.

He has forbidden his Governors to pass Laws of immediate and pressing importance, unless suspended in their operation till his Assent should be obtained; and when so suspended, he has utterly neglected to attend to them.

He has refused to pass other Laws for the accommodation of large districts of people, unless those people would relinquish the right of Representation in the Legislature, a right inestimable to them and formidable to tyrants only.

He has called together legislative bodies at places unusual, uncomfortable, and distant from the depository of their public Records, for the sole purpose of fatiguing them into compliance with his measures.

He has dissolved Representative Houses repeatedly, for opposing with manly firmness his invasions on the rights of the people.

He has refused for a long time, after such dissolutions, to cause others to be elected; whereby the Legislative powers, incapable of Annihilation, have returned to the People at large for their exercise; the State remaining in the mean time exposed to all the dangers of invasion from without, and convulsions within.

He has endeavoured to prevent the population of these States; for that purpose obstructing the Laws for Naturalization of Foreigners; refusing to pass others to encourage their migrations hither, and raising the conditions of new Appropriations of Lands.

He has obstructed the Administration of Justice, by refusing his Assent to Laws for establishing Judiciary powers.

He has made Judges dependent on his Will alone, for the tenure of their offices, and the amount and payment of their salaries.

He has erected a multitude of New Offices, and sent hither swarms of Officers to harrass our people, and eat out their substance.

He has kept among us, in times of peace, Standing Armies without the Consent of our legislatures.

He has affected to render the Military independent of and superior to the Civil power.

He has combined with others to subject us to a jurisdiction foreign to our constitution, and unacknowledged by our laws; giving his Assent to their Acts of pretended Legislation:
For Quartering large bodies of armed troops among us:

For protecting them, by a mock Trial, from punishment for any Murders which they should commit on the Inhabitants of these States:

For cutting off our Trade with all parts of the world:

For imposing Taxes on us without our Consent: For depriving us in many cases, of the benefits of Trial by Jury:

For transporting us beyond Seas to be tried for pretended offences.

For abolishing the free System of English Laws in a neighbouring Province, establishing therein an Arbitrary government, and enlarging its Boundaries so as to render it at once an example and fit instrument for introducing the same absolute rule into these Colonies:

For taking away our Charters, abolishing our most valuable Laws, and altering fundamentally the Forms of our Governments:

For suspending our own Legislatures, and declaring themselves invested with power to legislate for us in all cases whatsoever.

He has abdicated Government here, by declaring us out of his Protection and waging War against us.

He has plundered our seas, ravaged our Coasts, burnt our towns, and destroyed the lives of our people.

He is at this time transporting large Armies of foreign Mercenaries to compleat the works of death, desolation and tyranny, already begun with circumstances of Cruelty & perfidy scarcely paralleled in the most barbarous ages, and totally unworthy the Head of a civilized nation.

He has constrained our fellow Citizens taken Captive on the high Seas to bear Arms against their Country, to become the executioners of their friends and Brethren, or to fall themselves by their Hands.

He has excited domestic insurrections amongst us, and has endeavoured to bring on the inhabitants of our frontiers, the merciless Indian Savages, whose known rule of warfare, is an undistinguished destruction of all ages, sexes and conditions.

In every stage of these Oppressions We have Petitioned for Redress in the most humble terms: Our repeated Petitions have been answered only by repeated injury. A Prince whose character is thus marked by every act which may define a Tyrant, is unfit to be the ruler of a free people.

Nor have We been wanting in attentions to our Brittish brethren. We have warned them from time to time of attempts by their legislature to extend an unwarrantable jurisdiction over us. We have reminded them of the circumstances of our emigration and settlement here. We have appealed to their native justice and magnanimity, and we have conjured them by the ties of our common kindred to disavow these usurpations, which, would inevitably interrupt our connections and correspondence. They too have been deaf to the voice of justice and of consanguinity.

SIGNERS OF THE DECLARATION OF INDEPENDENCE

Georgia: Button Gwinnett, Lyman Hall, George Walton
North Carolina: William Hooper, Joseph Hewes, John Penn
South Carolina: Edward Rutledge, Thomas Heyward, Jr.,
Thomas Lynch, Jr., Arthur Middleton
Massachusetts: Samuel Adams, John Adams, Robert Treat Paine,
Elbridge Gerry, John Hancock
Maryland: Samuel Chase, William Paca, Thomas Stone,
Charles Carroll of Carrollton
Virginia: George Wythe, Richard Henry Lee, Thomas Jefferson,
Benjamin Harrison, Thomas Nelson, Jr., Francis Lightfoot Lee,
Carter Braxton
Pennsylvania: Robert Morris, Benjamin Rush, Benjamin Franklin,
John Morton, George Clymer, James Smith, George Taylor,
James Wilson, George Ross
Delaware: Caesar Rodney, George Read, Thomas McKean
New York: William Floyd, Philip Livingston, Francis Lewis,
Lewis Morris
New Jersey: Richard Stockton, John Witherspoon,
Francis Hopkinson, John Hart, Abraham Clark
New Hampshire: Josiah Bartlett, Matthew Thornton,
William Whipple
Rhode Island: Stephen Hopkins, William Ellery
Connecticut: Roger Sherman, Samuel Huntington,
William Williams, Oliver Wolcot

PRESIDENTS OF THE UNITED STATES

1	George Washington	1789-1797	24	Grover Cleveland	1893-1897
2	John Adams	1797-1801	25	William McKinley	1897-1901
3	Thomas Jefferson	1801-1809	26	Theodore Roosevelt	1901-1909
4	James Madison	1809-1817	27	William Howard Taft	1909-1913
5	James Monroe	1817-1825	28	Woodrow Wilson	1913-1921
6	John Quincy Adams	1825-1829	29	Warren G. Harding	1921-1923
7	Andrew Jackson	1829-1837	30	Calvin Coolidge	1923-1929
8	Martin Van Buren	1837-1841	31	Hebert Hoover	1929-1933
9	William Henry Harrison	1841-1841	32	Franklin D. Roosevelt	1933-1945
10	John Tyler	1841-1845	33	Harry S. Truman	1945-1953
11	James K. Polk	1845-1849	34	Dwight D. Eisenhower	1953-1961
12	Zachary Taylor	1849-1850	35	John F. Kennedy	1961-1963
13	Millard Fillmore	1850-1853	36	Lyndon B. Johnson	1963-1969
14	Franklin Pierce	1853-1857	37	Richard Nixon	1969-1974
15	James Buchanan	1857-1861	38	Gerald Ford	1974-1977
16	Abraham Lincoln	1861-1865	39	Jimmy Carter	1977-1981
17	Andrew Johnson	1865-1869	40	Ronald Reagan	1981-1989
18	Ulysses S. Grant	1869-1877	41	George H. W. Bush	1989-1993
19	Rutherford B. Hayes	1877-1881	42	Bill Clinton	1993-2001
20	James A. Garfield	1881-1881	43	George W. Bush	2001-2009
21	Chester A. Arthur	1881-1885	44	Barack Obama	2009-2017
22	Grover Cleveland	1885-1889	45	Donald Trump	2017-2021
23	Benjamin Harrison	1889-1893	46	Joe Biden	2021-

PLEDGE OF ALLEGIANCE
1954 (current) version

"I pledge allegiance to the Flag
Of the United States of America,
And to the Republic
For which it stands,
One Nation under God,
Indivisible,
with liberty and justice for all."

CHAPTER SIX

Workbook Section

U.S. Constitution Questions

Preamble to the U.S. Constitution – fill in blanks

Amendments Questions

Amendments/Bill of Rights Match

Facts to Memorize

KEYS (Answers)

Glossary

U.S. CONSTITUTION QUESTIONS

(Answers on Page 121)

ARTICLE 1-7

1. What are the two powers of Government? _____ and
_____ *(Page 13 - Article 1, Section 1)*

2. How many years do members of the House of Representatives get elected for?
_____. *(Page 13 - Article 1, Section 2, Clause 1)*

3. To be elected to the House of Representatives, you must be at least _____
years old, and have been a citizen of the U.S. for at least _____ years.
(Page 14 - Article 1, Section 2, Clause 2)

4. What is **the term used** for how Americans are counted (every ten years) to help
determine taxes by population growth? _____.
(Page 15 - Article 1, Section 2, Clause 3).

5. Who has the power to Impeach? *(Page 16 - Article 1, Section 2, Clause 5)*
a. Senate
b. House of Representatives

6. How many Senators are elected from each State? _____
How long do Senators serve? _____
How many Votes does each Senator have? _____
(Page 17 - Article 1, Section 3, Clause 1).

7. A Senator can serve a _____ year term. *(Page 18 - Article 1, Section 3, Clause 2).*

8. How old must a Senator be to be elected? _____. *(Page 18-Article 1, Section 3, Clause 3).*

9. Where does a Bill go once it is passed by the House and Senate in order to become Law? _____. *(Page ??, Article 1, Section 7, Clause 2).*

10. What is it called when the President will not sign a Bill? _____.
    (Page 24 - Article 1, Section 7, Clause 3).

11. What areas does Congress have power in Article 1, Section 8, Clause 1-3 to do?
    (Page 27)
    a. Power to Tax
    b. Power to Spend and Borrow
    c. Power to Make an Executive Order
    d. Power to Regulate Commerce

12. **What Clause** in Article 1, Section 8 gives Congress the power to make rules for Citizenship and Bankruptcy Laws? **Clause**_____.

13. The **Writ of Habeas Corpus** protects the right of unlawful _____.
    (Page 27 - Article 1, Section 9, Clause 2).

14. The term _____ means that if you did something that was legal at the time, but then it changed to be illegal, you can **NOT** be found guilty of that crime.
    (Page 34 - Article 1, Section 9, Clause 3).

15. How long is the **term** of an elected President and Vice President? _____.
    (Page 39 - Article 2, Section 1, Clause 1).

16. The President of the U.S. must be a U.S. Citizen, at least _____ years old, and have lived in the United States at least _____ years or more.
    (Page 42 - Article 2, Section 1, Clause 5).

17. Fill in the blanks for the President's Oath of Office: "I promise most sincerely and _____ that I will do my _____ as president of the United States, and I will, to the _____ _____ _____ _____, keep, protect and _____ the Constitution of the United States."
(Page 44 - Article 2, Section 1, Clause 8).

18. Who is the Commander-in-Chief in charge of the Military? _____.
(Page 44 - Article 2, Section 2, Clause 1).

19. What is the highest Court? _____.
(Page 48 - Article 3, Section 1).

20. What Court does a case that has been heard then appealed go to? _____. *(Page 50 - Article 3, Section 2, Clause 2).*

21. What is it called to change the Constitution? _____.
(Page 55 - Article 5).

22. What month, day, and year was the U.S. Constitution signed?_____.
(Page 58 - Article 7).

23. How many Articles of the U.S. Constitution are there? _____.

24. Who was the Signer of the Constitution from New York? _____. *(Page 59).*

PREAMBLE TO THE U.S. CONSTITUTION
Fill in the Blanks
(Answers on Page 122)

We, the _____ of the _____ States,

in Order to _____ a more perfect _____,

establish _____,

insure _____ Tranquility,

provide _____ the common _____,

promote the _____ Welfare,

and _____ the _____ of Liberty

to _____ and _____ Posterity,

do _____ and _____this Constitution

for the United _____ of _____."

AMENDMENTS QUESTIONS

(Answers on Page 123)

1. How many Amendments are there in the U.S. Constitution? _____.
   (Page 63).

2. What are the **first ten** Amendments called? _____.
   (Page 64).

3. What are the **five rights** that are found in Amendment One? *(Page 64 - Amendment 1).*

   _____

   _____

   _____

   _____

   _____

4. By law, I have the right to protect myself to keep and bear _____ (own a gun).
   (Page 65 -Amendment 2).

5. Soldiers can reside in my home without my permission in time of war?
   True   False   *(Page 65 - Amendment 3).*

6. The two things needed to search or seize my property are: _____
   _____.
   (Page 66 - Amendment 4).

7. I can't be forced to say that I am guilty of a crime. That is _____
   (Page 67 - Amendment 5).

8. If I am accused of a crime, I must be told why, and I have a right to a _____ _____.

   (Page 68 - Amendment 6).

9. Civil cases, not just Criminal, also have a right to _____.
   (Page 69 - Amendment 7).

10. When charged with a crime, I cannot receive Cruel and _____ Punishment, and fines or bail cannot be _____.
    (Page 70 - Amendment 8).

11. Some rights that aren't listed in the Constitution still must not be _____.
    (Page 71 - Amendment 9).

12. Powers that are not listed in the Constitution belongs to the _____.
    (Page 71 - Amendment 10).

13. If one State wants to sue another State, then the Federal courts get involved.
    True   False
    (Page 72 - Amendment 11).

14. According to Amendment 12, the President and Vice President cannot be from the _____.

    (Page 73 - Amendment 12).

15. Amendment 13 abolished _____.
    (Page 75 - Amendment 13).

16. Without due process, these three rights cannot be taken away?

    _____, _____, _____.

    (Page 76 - Amendment 14, Section 1).

17. Number of Representatives in the House is based on the number of people in each

_____.

(Page 77 - Amendment 14, Section 2).

18. No citizen can be denied the right to vote because of their _____ or

_____. *(Page 80 - Amendment 15).*

19. Amendment 16 gives Congress the power to _____ its citizens.
   (Page 80 - Amendment 16).

20. There are _____ Senators from each State, elected by the People every

_____ years. *(Page 81 – Amendment 17).*

21. Amendment 18 prohibited the use of _____.
   (Page 82, Amendment 18, Section 1).

22. Amendment 19 gave voting rights to _____ in the year_____.
   (Page 84 - Amendment 19).

23. When does the President's term end? _____.
   (Page 84, Amendment 20, Section 1).

24. What did Amendment 21 make legal again? _____.
   (Page 84 - Amendment 21).

25. How many terms can the President serve? _____.
   (Page 88 - Amendment 22, Section 1).

26. The District of Columbia was given the right to vote for _____.
   (Page 89 - Amendment 23, Section 1).

27. According to Amendment 24, a citizen cannot be made to do these two things:

_____

and _____.

(Page 90 - Amendment 24, Section 1).

28. Who becomes President if the President dies? _____.
    (Page 91 - Amendment 25, Section 1).

29. How old can you be to vote (minimum age)? _____.
    (Page 94 - Amendment 26, Section 1).

30. A member of Congress needs to wait to get a raise until the next election?
    True   False
    (Page 94 - Amendment 27).

AMENDMENTS /
BILL OF RIGHTS MATCH

(Find answers on Page 124)

Amendments	Letter (from below)
Amendment 1	
Amendment 2	
Amendment 3	
Amendment 4	
Amendment 5	
Amendment 6	
Amendment 7	
Amendment 8	
Amendment 9	
Amendment 10	

a. Privacy Rights (Search or Seize)

b. Powers by the States and People

c. Bails, Fines, Punishments

d. Individual Freedoms (Religion, Speech, Press, Assemble, Petition)

e. Rights Retained by the People

f. Right to Self-Defense (Bear Arms)

g. Rights in Civil Cases

h. Housing of Soldiers

i. Rights for a Fair Trial

j. Rights of Individuals in Criminal Cases

FACTS TO MEMORIZE

September Seventeenth, hooray,
It's U.S. Constitution Day!

September 17th

Eighteen sixty-five, we adore,
For slavery will be no more!

1865

In nineteen twenty women got,
The right to vote, for which they fought!

1920

Fifty-two words for me to ramble,
Fifty-two words in the Preamble!

52

Senators, touch your ears,
You're elected for 6 years!

7 Articles in the car,
7 Articles there are!

27 cats on the fence,
27 Amendments!

Freedom of Speech is so much fun.
It's found in Amendment One!

Hey, you Soldiers, go away,
Amendment Three says you can't stay!

Look **4** your Warrant to search me,

Or to take my property!
4ᵗʰ Amendment

Amendment Five - double jeopardy,
For the same crime, you can't charge me!
5ᵗʰ Amendment

As the Supreme Law of the Land,
The Constitution is so Grand!

KEY
U.S. CONSTITUTION QUESTIONS
(from page 107-109)

1. Senate, House of Representatives (or "House")
2. 2
3. 25, 7
4. Census
5. b
6. 2, 6 years, 1
7. 6
8. Over 30
9. The President
10. Veto
11. a,b,d
12. 4
13. Imprisonment
14. Ex Post Facto
15. 4 years
16. 35 years old, 14 years or more
17. Truthfully, job, best of my ability, defend
18. President
19. Supreme Court
20. U.S. Supreme Court
21. Amendment
22. September 17, 1787
23. 7
24. Alexander Hamilton

KEY
PREAMBLE TO THE U.S. CONSTITUTION
(from page 110)

We, the __People__ of the __United__ States,

in Order to __form__ a more perfect __Union__ ,

establish __Justice__ ,

insure __domestic__ Tranquility,

provide __for__ the common __defense__ ,

promote the __general__ Welfare,

and __secure__ the __Blessings__ of Liberty

to __ourselves__ and __our__ Posterity,

do __ordain__ and __establish__ this Constitution

for the United __States__ of __America__ ."

KEY
AMENDMENTS QUESTIONS
(from page 111-114)

1. 27
2. Bill of Rights
3. Freedom of Religion, speech, Press, Assemble, Petition
4. Arms
5. False
6. Self-Incrimination
7. A Warrant and Good Cause
8. Fair, speedy public trial
9. A Trial
10. Unusual, Excessively high
11. Denied
12. States
13. False
14. Same State
15. Slavery
16. Life, Liberty, Property
17. State
18. Race or Color
19. Tax
20. Two, Six
21. Alcohol
22. Women, 1920
23. January 20th
24. Alcohol
25. Two
26. President
27. Pay a voting tax, Take a reading test to vote
28. The Vice President
29. 18
30. True

KEY
AMENDMENTS /
BILL OF RIGHTS MATCH
(from page 115)

Amendments	Letter (from below)
Amendment 1	d
Amendment 2	f
Amendment 3	h
Amendment 4	a
Amendment 5	j
Amendment 6	i
Amendment 7	g
Amendment 8	c
Amendment 9	e
Amendment 10	b

a. Privacy Rights (Search or Seize)

b. Powers by the States and People

c. Bails, Fines, Punishments

d. Individual Freedoms (Religion, Speech, Press, Assemble, Petition)

e. Rights Retained by the People

f. Right to Self-Defense (Bear Arms)

g. Rights in Civil Cases

h. Housing of Soldiers

i. Rights for a Fair Trial

j. Rights of Individuals in Criminal Cases

GLOSSARY
U.S. Constitution and Government Terms

A

Amend – To change the wording or meaning of a motion, bill, Constitution, etc. by formal procedure. For example, Congress may amend the Constitution.

Amendment - A proposal by a Member (in committee or floor session of the respective Chamber) to alter the language or provisions of a bill or act. It is voted on in the same manner as a bill. The Constitution of the United States, as provided in Article 5, may be amended when two-thirds of each House of Congress approves a proposed amendment and three-fourths of the states thereafter ratify it.

American Revolutionary War - The war in which the United States won independence from Great Britain (1775-1783).

Article – One section of a U.S. state or federal constitution defined by topic.

Articles of Confederation - The first constitution of the 13 American states. They were written in 1777, adopted in 1781, but then replaced in 1787 by the Constitution of the United States.

B

Bill - Formally introduced legislation. Most legislative proposals are in the form of bills and are designated as H.R. (House of Representatives) or S. (Senate), depending on the House in which they are introduced.

Bill of Rights - The first ten amendments to the United States Constitution.

Branches of Government – Three "branches of government", separation of powers. Legislative (makes laws – Congress, comprised of the House of Representatives and Senate); Executive (carries out laws – President, Vice President, Cabinet, most Federal agencies); Judicial (evaluates laws – Supreme Court and other courts).

C

Cabinet - A group of governmental officials who head various departments in the Executive Branch and advise the president.

Census - An official count of the number of persons living in a geographic area, such as a city, county, state, or nation.

Centralized Government - A form of government in which the national government maintains the power.

Checks and Balances - Limits placed on the branches of Government by giving each the right to amend acts of the other branches.

Citizen - A native or naturalized subject of a state or nation who owes allegiance to its government and is entitled to its protection.

Colonist - Someone living in a colony.

Commerce - Buying and selling of goods; it is usually thought of as trade between states or nations.

Committee - A group of Members of Congress appointed to investigate, debate, and report on legislation.

Congress - The seat of legislative power.

Constitution - The document which establishes the basic principles of the American Government.

E

Electoral College - The name for the "indirect" process by which the people elect the president. The "electors" are determined by the number of representatives each state (including Washington, D.C.) has in the House of Representatives and Senate. In a presidential election year the "electors" meet in their respective state capitals on the first Monday after the second Wednesday to "vote" for the President.

Executive branch - One of the three branches of our government with the purpose of enforcing laws.

Express Powers - Powers specifically granted to the federal government as enumerated in Article I, Section 8 of the Constitution.

F

Federal - A union of groups or states in which each member agrees to give up some of its governmental power in certain areas to a central authority; in the United States, it is used to describe the central Government.

Founding Fathers - Important leaders who took part in the American Revolution and helped form our system of Government. George Washington, Thomas Jefferson, Benjamin Franklin, James Madison, and John Adams are considered Founding Fathers.

H

House of Representatives - Along with the Senate, it is one of the two Houses of the U.S. Congress. Members are granted to each state based upon population and each representative serves a two-year term.

I

Impeachment - A Constitutional "check" the Congress has on the President or other high federal officials. It involves an accusation against that official.

Inalienable Rights - The natural rights of all men defined by John Locke as life, liberty, and property that can only be taken away by God. Government is created to protect these rights.

J

Judge – A public official appointed to decide cases in a court of law.

Judicial Branch - One of the three branches of our government with the purpose of interpreting laws.

Jury – A body of people (typically twelve in number) sworn to give a verdict in a legal case on the basis of evidence submitted to them in court.

Justice – The quality of being fair, reasonable, or impartial.

L
Law - A system of rules of conduct established and enforced by the authority, legislation, or custom of a given community, state, or nation. Used in the singular to mean a specific law (a law protecting free speech) or in the plural to refer to a set of laws (the law of the land).

Legislative Branch – Made up of the House and Senate, known collectively as the Congress.

Legislation - A law or a body (set) of laws.

Liberty – Freedom of choice

M
Majority – The greater number

O
Oath – Solemn promise. A sworn declaration that one will tell the truth.

P
Preamble - An introduction to a document.

President: A head of state that had been elected to office; also called chief executive. The President of the United States is the highest elected official in the nation and head of Government, the leader of the executive branch, and the commander-in-chief of the U.S. Armed Forces.

R
Ratification - In U.S. Government, this can be the act of approval of a proposed constitutional amendment by the legislatures of the States; it can also refer to the Senate process of advice and consent to treaties negotiated by the President.

Representative - A person appointed, chosen, or elected to act on another's behalf. In Congress, Representatives are granted to each state based upon population and each Representative serves a two-year term.

Republic - A state or nation in which the power rests in all the citizens entitled to vote and their elected representatives; a republic also has a President and not a king or other type of monarch.

Resolution - A proposal approved by either or both Houses of Congress which, except for joint resolutions signed by the President, does not have the force of law.

S

Senate - Along with the House of Representatives, it is one of the two Houses of the U.S. Congress. There are two Senators granted to each state and each Senator serves a six-year term. There are currently 100 members in the Senate.

Senator: The Constitution requires that a Senator be at least 30 years old, a citizen of the United States for at least nine years, and an inhabitant of the state from which he or she is elected. A person elected or appointed to the Senate and duly sworn is a Senator. There are currently 100 members in the Senate.

Separation of Powers - The system of dividing power and authority; in the United States, it is divided among the legislative, executive, and judicial branches of the Government.

Sovereign - Above or superior to all others; chief; greatest; supreme dominion or power.

T

Tax – Funds levied by the government on workers' income and business profits, or added to the cost of some goods, services, and transactions.

Term – A fixed or limited period of time.

Treason - Being unfaithful or disloyal to one's own country.

V

Veto - The procedure, as allowed by the Constitution, by which the President refuses to approve a bill or joint resolution and thus prevents its enactment into law.

Sources: *bensguide.gpo.gov, constitutionfacts.com*

May we, as Americans, love our country,
stand for freedom, know our rights,
and defend the U.S. Constitution,
is my hope and prayer.

Debbi S. Rollo

Contact Debbi at
drollo1787@gmail.com
www.readconstitution.com

You may also enjoy Volume 1
(A summarized version of the Constitution)
U.S. CONSTITUTION RHYMES
A Fun and Easy Way
To Learn and Love the Constitution

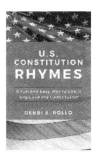

ON AMAZON!

Email Debbi at drollo1787@gmail.com
to be added to her Email List For News and
Updates about her books, events, and more.

Made in the USA
Columbia, SC
14 September 2024

41820954R00080